Silver Christmas Ornaments

Silver Christmas Ornaments

A Collectors' Guide

Clara Johnson Scroggins

San Diego • New York
A. S. Barnes & Company, Inc.
In London:
The Tantivy Press

First Edition
Manufactured in the United States of America

For information write to:

A. S. Barnes & Company, Inc.
P.O. Box 3051
La Jolla, California 92038

The Tantivy Press
Magdalen House
136-148 Tooley Street
London, SE1 2TT, England

Library of Congress Cataloging in Publication Data

Scroggins, Clara Johnson, 1931-
  Silver Christmas ornaments.
  Bibliography: p.
  Includes index.
  1. Christmas decorations—Collectors and collecting.
2. Silver articles—Collectors and collecting. I. Title.
TT900.C4S37   739.2′3′8′   79-15323
ISBN 0-498-02385-0

1 2 3 4 5 6 7 8 9   84 83 82 81 80

This book is dedicated to the memory of my parents, Hughey and Estelle Johnson;
to the entire Johnson clan: Precious, Doc, Hughey, Freddye Rose,
Charles, Maybelline, June, Vicki,
my granddaughter Michele, my godsons Aaron and Brian;
to lovers of the Christmas holiday season;
and most of all to my son Michael Watkins and my husband Joe.

Contents

Preface

It is not often that a serious collector of anything has the opportunity to start early enough to secure all of the important items he or she collects. In 1973 I met a guy, Joe, and bought a sterling "Christmas Cross" tree ornament (1973 issue) to commemorate this meeting. The following year I married Joe and bought the 1974 Reed & Barton "Christmas Cross" to commemorate that event. The four of us, along with about seven hundred limited and unlimited sterling, silver-plated, and vermeil Christmas ornaments are living "happily ever after."

It has been said that I collect any and everything, including "people," and that may be, in part, true, for in 1974 I felt my two initial "Christmas Crosses" would be lost on the tree of glass balls, antique ornaments, handmade ones, etc., so I decided to go back and purchase the earlier dated crosses and began to decorate a small tree with silver ornaments for the den. During and after the 1974 Christmas season, I pursued sterling and silver-plated ornaments with gusto! With the help of a half-price sale at David Harvey Jewelers in Norwalk, Connecticut, and owner Mrs. Harvey Rosemann, I started collecting, haphazardly, just to fill my tree. By January of 1975 I owned assorted manufacturers' ornaments in duplicate, triplicate, and more—no first editions and several editions missing in every collection.

I then decided it was time to sit down and create a ledger, listing the ornaments by manufacturer, collection names, and dates of issue, and fill in what I owned and what I needed to complete each collection. At Zantow Ferguson Jewelers in Stamford, aided by the owner, Carol F. Vesely and staff members, Jimmy Hughes, Mary Hughes, and Sarah Tyson, I methodically began completing my sets of Gorham snowflakes, icicles, unlimited collection and Gorham's American Heritage, Reed & Barton cross collection, Wallace collections of bells and doves, Lunt's trefoils, and Towle's twelve days.

To my dismay, the first Towle was at that time $150.00 (originally $10.00), the Wallace bell $150.00, the dove $80.00, Reed & Barton's cross $50.00, and Gorham's snowflake $60.00. Needless to say, I was not prepared nor did I expect to pay this kind of money for Christmas ornaments, but I did pay a deposit on the Towle and had it and many others on my 1975 tree.

Armed with a 1975 Christmas gift (a subscription to the *Antique Trader*) from friend Marianne Connon, I came in contact with dealers around the country, many of whom I consider friends and want to thank, such as Roy and Nans Shoults, "Albatross Antiques" in Manchester, New Hampshire; Steve Cooper and his father of

"Coopers Jewelers" in Sycamore, Illinois; Barbara Werick at the "Lower Plate" in Oklahoma City, Oklahoma; and Kathy Muselle of Rogers and Company in Mansfield, Ohio.

All are fine business firms who were willing to assist me in every way in finding the ornaments I needed. These and other dealers assured me I had the largest known, singly owned collection. My goal of not only completing my existing sets but also of obtaining every available ornament or set made was almost reached. I did then and still do buy ornaments all year long, justifying my purchases with "I'm not spending, I'm investing" and rightfully so because I discovered my collection grew rapidly and the value soared! By November of 1977 my collection had become so valuable and some ornaments so scarce that I needed to insure them before decorating my tree. My broker's face registered "shock" when I requested the insurance, but he finally decided I was not "crazy" and asked for a certified appraisal for consideration. It was my turn to be shocked, for the appraised bottom line figure could be a down payment on a house! Now my collection remains "housed" in a bank vault and I did get the insurance. I had pictures professionally done of my tree (for insurance) and copies were used at the display area of ornament dealers around the country and have been sent on request to the manufacturers.

I must purchase around 125 or more ornaments each year to keep my existing collection up-to-date and pray that no new collection is offered.

In my search for names and manufacturers, collections, issue dates, issue prices, availability, I found no *one* dealer carried all collections or knew of them all. For that reason this book has been written. To answer the what, when, where, why, and by whom these ornaments were made, limited or unlimited, sterling, plated, vermeil, issue prices, and in some cases, edition numbers for present and future collectors.

I will continue to collect and will update this book in the future. My sincere hope is that the future generations of my family will love and enjoy this collection, pass them on to their children and remember me each year as they decorate their Christmas trees.

"HAPPY HOLIDAYS—HAPPY HUNTING"

Acknowledgments

For their assistance in making this book possible I would like to thank David S. Parkinson of Gorham Silversmiths; Cindy Haskins, Ashton Edwards, and Stuart A. Young of International Silver Co.; Henry M. Tovar of Wallace Silver Co.; Norman Jubb and Reno Pisano of Towle Silversmiths; Patrice Johnson and Richard Gillespie of Reed and Barton; George C. Lunt and Bernice Erhardt of Lunt Silversmiths; Elaine McCoy and Art W. Kidd at Oneida; Robert F. Welzenback at Samuel Kirk and Son; Mildred Ritter and Ernest S. Quick at American Heritage Publishers; Frank Lewis and Richard B. Hamilton of Crest Fruit Co.; Pat Trush of Cazenovia Abroad, Ltd.; at the Lincoln Mint thanks to Marcia D. Scarborough; Brenda Vierthaler of Sterling Imports; Wessley Prothero at the Danbury Mint; John Reynolds of John-John Enterprises; Marian Puhle and Robert Johnston of Stieff Silver Co.; Shelia Hancock of the Franklin Mint; Nans and Roy Shoults of Albatross Antiques, Manchester, New Hampshire, Kathy Musille of Rogers and Co., Mansfield, Ohio; Barbara Weirick, Lower Plate, Oklahoma; Deanne Olinger, Halls of Kansas City; Stephen Smith, in Virginia; John Sanders, Anne Cron, and Dave Lewis at Cahners; the Harvey Rosemans, David Harvey Jewelers Inc.; Steve Cooper and Father at Coopers Jewelry in Sycamore, Illinois; Carol Ferguson Vesely, Mary Hughes, Jimmy Hughes, and Sarah Tyson at Zantow Ferguson Jewelers, Stamford, Connecticut; Joanne Levi, Kruckmeyer and Cohn; Cathy Cohen, Downs Collector Showcase; Cynthia Beneduce of the Metropolitan Museum of Art; Dayton Hudson Jewelers; and many more too numerous to mention.

"Hats off" to some of my collector friends who also assisted me: Thelma Hardiman and Cathryn Collins of Buffalo, New York; Steve Smith of Fairfax, Virginia; Margaret Strayhorne and Marianne Connon of Stamford, Connecticut; Kay Black of Stratford, Connecticut; Dorothy Robinson of Morrisville, Pennsylvania; Patricia Cronkright, Houston, Texas and the many other collectors, including those to whom I have given the "bug." Thanks also to Ann Cron for her valuable editorial assistance. Very special thanks to Patricia Fickett, my calm, untiring manuscript typist and Lucille Domigio, another typist; to Margaret Strayhorne, my good friend who helped in the editing; and to my husband Joe, who had to look at Christmas ornaments all around the house—all year long!

Introduction

Christmas is the happiest of all holiday seasons, a time of celebration, the birth of Christ, family gatherings, gift giving and receiving, and decorating the home and Christmas tree with bright new Christmas tree ornaments and those passed down from generation to generation.

In 1964, Halls of Kansas City, Missouri, a division of the Hallmark Card Company, contracted with the Webster Silver Co. (now defunct) to create exclusively for Halls, an annual sterling-silver bell, Christmas tree ornament, dated to commemorate the special happy memories of each Christmas season for those who purchased them. Following Halls in 1966, the Franklin Mint made available one thousand sets of the Twelve Days of Christmas and Cazenovia Abroad Ltd. offered their first ornaments. In 1970, Gorham Silver Co. issued their first snowflake and shortly after offerings were made by the Metropolitan Museum of Art, Wallace Silver Co., Reed and Barton, Towle, Oneida, Lunt, Kirk, International, American Heritage Publishing Co., Steiff, The Smithsonian, The Hamilton Mint, Danbury Mint, John-John Silver Co., Neiman Marcus, Dayton Hudson Jewelers, Frank Lewis, Leonard Silver Co., Lord and Taylor, Jana, and General Mills. New companies and collections were created for the 1978 Christmas season and at present there are more than one hundred collections and about seven hundred different ornaments available in limited and annual editions, created in sterling silver, silver plate, and vermeil.

This book is an attempt at recording them for the sake of manufacturers, mints, dealers, and collectors, and to record my own collection and the collection of my good friend, Stephan L. Smith and his family.

Silver Christmas Ornaments

— 1 —
The Gorham Collections

Sterling Christmas Ornament Collections—Snowflakes
Gorham's Collection—Pierced Collection—Icicles
Gorham's American Heritage Collection—Sterling Tree Topping

The Gorham Corporation, a division of Textron, was founded by Jabez Gorham around 1815. The company evolved through many partnerships and acquisitions before becoming what it is today. John Gorham, son of Jabez, joined his father in the company's early existence and introduced machine-made silverware. He designed much of the machinery himself, beginning a new era in the industry.

Gorham, a leader in the silver industry and noted for producing unexcelled flatware and holloware, led this industry into the "Limited" and/or "Annual" Christmas ornament era. Few companies made sterling or plated ornaments before the "boom" started by Gorham's 1970 limited-edition, annual sterling Snowflake. To date Gorham has produced a sterling Tree Topping and has begun five different collections, ending only one.

Thanks to David S. Parkinson, product manager of sterling and pewter holloware, for his capable assistance in gathering the following material about Gorham ornaments.

Sterling Snowflakes (Limited)

It has been said that no two snowflakes are alike; well, if that is so, the Snowflake collection can go on into infinity. Gorham's snowfall began with a first-edition, sterling Snowflake in 1970 and I suspect that the future generations of my family will have to complete this beautiful sterling "blizzard" for me.

Each year's edition since the 1970 Snowflake has been incomparable. The avalanche of designs by the Gorham designer, Richard Maiella, becomes more evident with each year's Snowflake.

There are to date six points to each multifaceted, intricate ornament. They are basically about the same size, except the first (1970) is slightly smaller. Each hollow ornament has a smooth-surfaced back with "Sterling," the date, and Gorham's markings stamped on it. This collection exemplifies the quality we have come to expect from Gorham.

The series of sterling Snowflakes was all designed by Richard Maiella. They all measure 3¼ inches in diameter. To quote Mr. Maiella, "Sterling ornaments have to reflect light to be effective. The Snowflakes were stylized and faceted in order to get the twinkle effect. I tried to relate one Snowflake to the other, so that when one has the complete set they appear to come from the same family. The problem is that we must make each Snowflake significantly different, yet maintain the family look."

1

Issue prices:
1970—$10.00
1971—$10.00
1972—$10.00
1973—$10.95

1974—$17.50
1975—$17.50
1976—$20.00
1977—$22.50
1978—$22.50
1979—$28.50

Icicles 1973–1974 (Limited)

The Icicle, a sterling, limited-edition ornament produced by Gorham, I suspect, is "the most limited ornament." The issue dates were 1973 and 1974 only. The issue number was only ten thousand per year. No change was made in its design, only in the date, in its two-year existence. The multifaceted ornament is about five inches from top to tip, starts wide at the top and tapers to a point (as icicles usually do). I have three in my collection and have scoured the country seeking more, but they are just not to be found, to my dismay.

I know other serious collectors who have never seen one! I understand they were slow sellers initially and by the time most collectors realized they were available, they were not. I do have a feeling they made their way to the melting pot and are a part of the "1975 Snowflake"! Mine are prized. Designer: Richard Maiella. Issue price: $10.00.

The Unlimited Collection

"Angel" 1972

After such tremendous success with their Snowflake, Gorham started another collection of finely crafted, sterling Christmas ornaments. In 1972 an "Angel" was issued as the "first" of this unlimited collection. She wears a floral sculptured robe, and her hands are clasped as if she is blessing all who gaze upon her. Her spread wings and her halo give her a background. Designer: Lucien Sermon. Dimensions: 4" h × 1½" w. Issue price: $17.50.

Gorham's First Edition "Snowflake"   *1970*
PHOTO BY GORHAM

Gorham's Second Edition "Snowflake"   *1971*
PHOTO BY GORHAM

Gorham's Fourth Edition "Snowflake"   *1973*
PHOTO BY GORHAM

Gorham's Fifth Edition "Snowflake"   *1974*
PHOTO BY GORHAM

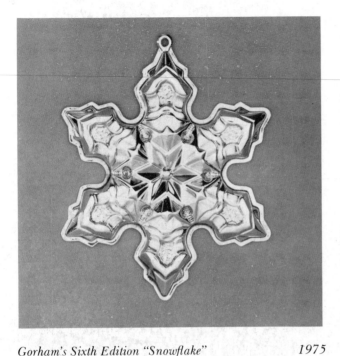

Gorham's Sixth Edition "Snowflake"   1975
PHOTO BY GORHAM

Gorham's Seventh Edition "Snowflake"   1976
PHOTO BY GORHAM

Gorham's Eighth Edition "Snowflake"   1977
PHOTO BY GORHAM

Gorham's Ninth Edition "Snowflake"   1978
PHOTO BY GORHAM

Gorham's Tenth Edition "Snowflake"   *1979*
PHOTO BY GORHAM

Gorham's Snowflake #1349   *1976*
PHOTO BY GORHAM

Gorham's Snowflake #1970 P   *1976*
PHOTO BY GORHAM

Gorham's "Icicle"   *1973–74*
PHOTO BY GORHAM

"Three Wise Men" 1973

"Three Wise Men" or the three kings of the Orient are bearing gifts for the new-born King they are seeking. You can *feel* the designs in their royal robes, the tasseled sash, the points and peaks in the crown, and their finely etched beards and facial expressions. Hats off to the designer staff at Gorham for this 1973 offering. Designer: Lucien Sermon. Dimensions: 3¼" h × 1⅞" w. Issue price: $17.50.

"Drummer Boy" 1974

The "Drummer Boy" made his debut in 1974. Appearing freshly groomed and standing erect in his uniform with all the trappings, he is ready to beat his three-dimensional drum and join the parade! Designer: Lucien Sermon. Dimensions: 4" h × 1¼" w. Issue price: $20.00.

"Snowman" 1975

The "Snowman" was designed and offered in 1975. Looking like the "Snowman" I have always wanted to build (and couldn't) he dons a rakish top hat with holly balls and leaves in its hand, has a long, fringed scarf wrapped around his neck, wears mittens, and in his right hand he holds a broom that extends over his shoulder. He has a round nose, button eyes, a silly smile on his face, and of course a corncob pipe stuck in his mouth. *Adorable!* Designer: Lucien Sermon. Dimensions: 3½" h × 1½" w. Issue price: $20.00.

"Santa" 1976

Jolly old "Santa" came out at Christmas time, 1976, as he does every year, only this time he is a "sterling idea" executed by the Gorham craftsmen. He is just as I imagine him to be—jolly, fat, bearded, and wearing "his uniform," with his "goodie bag" thrown over his shoulder. Designer: Lucien Sermon. Dimensions: 3¾" h × 1⅞" w. Issue price: $20.00.

Gorham's "Wise Men"   1973
"Angel"   1972
PHOTO BY GORHAM

Gorham's "Drummer Boy"   1974
PHOTO BY GORHAM

Gorham's "Snowman"   *1975*
PHOTO BY GORHAM

Gorham's "Santa's Helper"   *1977*
PHOTO BY GORHAM

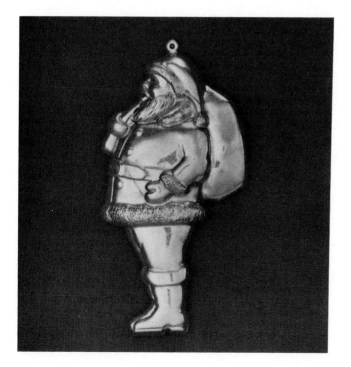

Gorham's "Santa Claus"   *1976*
PHOTO BY GORHAM

"Elf" "Santa's Helper" 1977

An "Elf" "Santa's Helper", made a showing in 1977. Santa has been known to be bogged down with filling orders, and I understand that at the north pole he has a shop with lots of elves busily working all year long to make the toys that little children dream of finding under the tree on Christmas morn. This helper, looking like a typical elf, is wearing an apron with a pocket filled with tools and is carrying a beautiful Christmas tree ball ornament that is so large that it dwarfs him. I would love it if I could find an ornament like it for my tree. Gorham, are you listening? Designer: Judy Lee. Dimensions: 4″ h × 2⅜″ w. Issue price: $20.00.

"Waiting for Christmas" 1978

The fall of each year finds me shopping and planning and "Waiting for Christmas," and that's the subject of the 1978 issue of this collection.

Three little children, standing in a row, dressed in their nighties, are ready to be tucked in bed so Santa can make his rounds. The two girls and a boy, shown in graduated heights, are "Waiting for Christmas." One girl holds a night candle, the other cuddles her doll, and the little boy holds on to his sister. Designer: Richard Maiella. Dimensions: 3⅛″ h × 2″ w. Issue price: $20.00.

"Choirboys" 1979

Two "Choirboys," dressed in their choir robes, faces shining clean and hair neatly groomed, are standing, holding their choir books and caroling. Dimension: 3″ h. Issue price: $22.50.

Prices on all 1979 ornaments were unstable because of unstable silver prices.

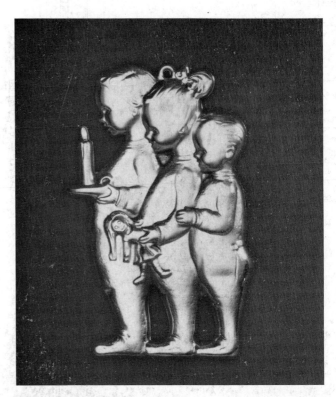

Gorham's "Waiting for Christmas"   *1978*
PHOTO BY GORHAM

Gorham's American Heritage Collection (Unlimited)

The Gorham Silversmith Company was commissioned to make sterling silver Christmas ornaments for American Heritage Publishers, to be issued one annually by the publishers, issues starting in 1972. Gorham gained permission to reproduce and issue this collection; each Gorham ornament is issued one year after the American Heritage offering. In 1973, Gorham's first of this collection was the "Mount Vernon Peace Dove," the same as offered by the publishers in 1972.

"Mount Vernon Peace Dove" 1973 (Sterling)

The 1973 "Mount Vernon Peace Dove" is a sleek contemporary beauty with its wings spread in flight and a branch in its beak, a fitting beginning for this collection and the 1973 holiday tree. Dimensions: 4¼″ h × 3½″ w. Issue price: $20.00.

Gorham's "Choir Boys"   *1979*
PHOTO BY GORHAM

"Christmas Reindeer" 1974

To usher in the 1974 holiday season, a graceful "Christmas Reindeer" was the second issue. He is four-pointed, designed in motion, and somehow you know Rudolph is just ahead and Santa in his sleigh is bringing up the rear. Dimensions: 3¾″ h × 2⅞″ w. Issue price: $25.00.

"Angel with Trumpet" 1975

A Christmas "Angel with Trumpet." She seems to be hovering in the air and heralding the coming of the Christmas day. Dimensions: 5″ h × 2½″ w. Issue price: $25.00.

American Heritage Dove   First Edition
Introduced in Gorham's Line in 1973.
PHOTO BY GORHAM

American Heritage Reindeer   Second Edition
By Gorham 1974.
PHOTO BY GORHAM

9

American Heritage Angel   Third Edition
By Gorham 1975.
PHOTO BY GORHAM

"Locomotive" 1976

The beautifully detailed, old-fashioned "Locomotive" of 1976 is reminiscent of our country's early modes of transportation and brings us down out of the skies to our bicentennial celebration. Dimensions: $4^3/_{16}''$ h × 2″ w. Issue price: $25.00.

"St. Nicholas" 1977

In some European countries "St. Nicholas" not only brought the toys to all the good girls and boys, he also brought the tree. The 1977 "St. Nicholas' " back is laden with a bag of toys and gifts and the "Tannenbaum" on his shoulder. Dimensions: 4″ h × 2¾″ w. Issue price: $25.00.

"Round the Tree" 1978

Children "Round the Tree" is the 1978 member of this collection, a towering, lovely decorated tree, with four happy children holding hands and dancing around it. A banner at their feet wishes all a "MERRY CHRISTMAS."

This collection is all sterling, hollow, and evokes Christmas past. For a sneak peek into the collection, 1979, see the American Heritage Society's own 1978 offering. Dimensions: 3½″ h × 2⅜″ w. Issue price: $25.00.

(Drawings by Lucien Sermon on entire "American Heritage" collection.)

American Heritage Locomotive   Fourth Edition
By Gorham 1976.
PHOTO BY GORHAM

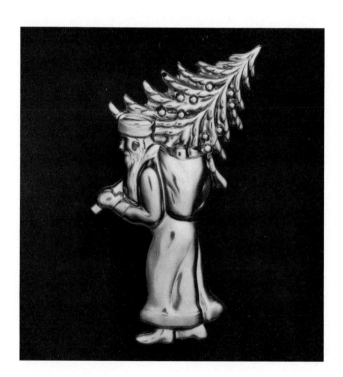

American Heritage St. Nick   Fifth Edition
By Gorham 1977.
PHOTO BY GORHAM

American Heritage Round-The-Tree   Sixth Edition
By Gorham 1978
PHOTO BY GORHAM

11

"Santa and his Sled" 1979

The Pierced Collection (Unlimited)

A sterling Santa and his gift-laden sled arrived in 1979 pulled by one reindeer! I wonder if that means that Santa also had a fuel shortage? The 4 inch long ornament was issued early in the fall. Issue price: $27.50.

For the 1977 Christmas season Gorham created and issued four new, three-dimensional sterling, open or lacy ornaments.

1. A "Lantern" centered with a flaming candle. It has a cage look with vines intertwined throughout and stars at the top. 1977. Designer: Robert McCutcheon. Dimensions: 3½″ h × 2½″ w. Issue price: $15.00.
2. A "Christmas Tree" with cut designs of ornaments, Santa's sleigh, peace dove, angel, stars, bells, and candy canes. 1977. Designer: Robert McCutcheon. Dimensions: 3¾″ h × 3⅛″ w. Issue price: $15.00.
3. "Turtle Doves," kissing, in their own lover's cage. 1977. Designer: Robert McCutcheon. Dimensions: 3¼″ h × 2½″ w. Issue price: $15.00.
4. A "Christmas Tree Ball" with cut designs of stars, angels, bells, doves, and noel. 1977. Designer: Robert McCutcheon. Dimensions: 2½″ h × 2¾″ w. Issue price: $15.00.
The 1977 "Tree" was issued again in 1978. Designer: Robert McCutcheon. Dimensions: 3¾″ h × 3⅛″ w. Issue price: $15.00.

American Heritage Santa in His Sled   Seventh Edition By Gorham 1979
PHOTO BY GORHAM

Gorham's *"Christmas Tree"*   *1977 & 1978*
PHOTO BY GORHAM

Gorham's *"Turtle Dove"*   *1976*
PHOTO BY GORHAM

Gorham's *"Christmas Ball"* 1977
PHOTO BY GORHAM

Gorham's *"Lantern"*   *1977*
PHOTO BY GORHAM

1979 Pierced Collection

(1) A "Carousel" with a domed, gingerbread-designed top, five ornately saddled horses galloping around and around, and "We wish you a Merry Christmas and a Happy New Year" bannered around the bottom. Dimensions: 2⅞" h × 2" w. Issue price: fluctuated with price of sterling from $22.50 to $32.50.

(2) A "Treasure Chest" shaped similar to the postal box on the street corner. It represents the three kinds and their gifts. Cutout bust design of the three kings are shown on three sides with their gifts of "Gold," "Frankincense" and "Myrrh" just above their crowns. On the fourth side is a camel representing the transportation for their journey to Bethlehem. Dimensions: 2⅝" square, 3" h. Issue price: $22.50 to $32.50.

(3) A "Rocking Horse" in three dimensions looks as if he simply stepped off the carousel and grew a wee bit. He is on rockers that say "Seaons Greetings." Dimensions: 3½" h × 3½" w from nose to tail. Issue price: $22.50 to $32.50.

(4) The only dated ornament in this pierced group is the "Steam Engine." The old-fashioned steam engine says "NOEL," is decorated with holly leaves and dated 1979. Like the others in this collection it is marked "Gorham Sterling." It is coated and will need to be polished. Dimensions: 2⅓" h × 4" long. Issue price: $22.50 to $32.50.

Gorham's "Carousel"   *1979*
PHOTO BY GORHAM

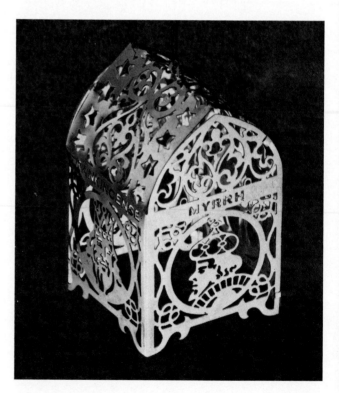

Gorham's "Treasure Chest"   *1979*
PHOTO BY GORHAM

Tree Topping

Gorham tops off their collections with a tree topping for your collection and tree. It is a sterling cross with a sunburst design at the top. A fitting way to top your sterling tree. Designer: J. Russell Price, past director of design. Dimension: 7¼″ h. Issue price: $16.50.

Gorham's "Rocking Horse"   *1979*
PHOTO BY GORHAM

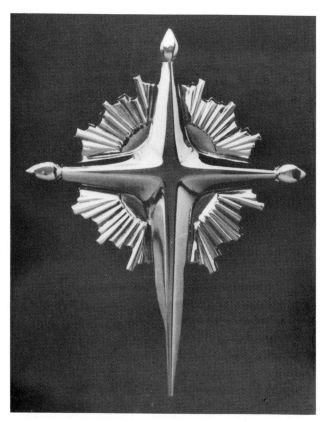

Gorham's "Steam Engine"   *1979*
PHOTO BY GORHAM

Gorham's Tree Topper—Sunburst Cross
PHOTO BY GORHAM

─── 2 ───
The Towle Silversmiths Collections

The Twelve Days of Christmas
and
Christmas Melodies Medallions

The Towle Manufacturing Company, known for fine silver craftsmanship since 1690, has immortalized a favorite Christmas carol, "The Twelve Days of Christmas," with a sterling-silver, medallion ornament collection. Starting in 1971, the company has issued and anticipates continuing to issue the twelve days of Christmas, keeping in the tradition of the song, one ornament issued each year, completing the set by 1982. Each ornament is copywrited, dated, and beautifully designed (1972–1978) by Ted Merry, a member of the silversmiths' staff at Towle. After each year's production is completed, the dies are destroyed or retired, never to be used again.

The method for making these medallions is by the direct reverse cutting in steel of the striking die by hand. The cutting of this die is done by the designer/craftsman himself who searches the final solution in process.

Towle's Twelve Days Medallions have proven to be one of the favorites of collectors.

Towle's second collection called "Christmas Melodies Medallions" started in 1978 depicting Christmas carols. The first issue is "Silent Night, Holy Night."

Towle's 1978 First Edition   "Christmas Melodies"
PHOTO BY TOWLE

"The Twelve Days of Christmas"

"Partridge in a Pear Tree"
(first edition—first day)

"A Partridge in a Pear Tree", the first edition issued in 1971 at $10.00 is being sold at the time of this writing for as much as $650.00, if you can find it. This disc-shaped ornament is actually two discs fused together with hammered finished edges. On one side is a "raised" designed pear tree with a partridge perched on a branch. A

16

Towle's 1979 Second Edition "Christmas Melodies"
"Deck the Halls with Boughs of Holly"
PHOTO BY TOWLE

Towle's 1971   First Edition "Partridge in a
Pear Tree"
PHOTO BY TOWLE

peace dove with a flower in its beak is featured on the other side. Designer: Greenleaf Martin. Dimensions: 2½" h × 2½" w.

Because of the scarcity and soaring price of this first-edition ornament at the time I purchased mine, I had to pay monthly installments to buy it. It commanded the top position on the tree that year and I remember staring at it for hours.

"Two Turtle Doves"
(second edition — second day)

The second day of Christmas medallion has now joined the ranks of the "scarce" ornaments and is, needless to say, expensive! "Two Turtle Doves" perched on ornately designed branches, all "raised" with three bordering ridges, are the main feature. The obverse side shows a baroque-designed cross encircled with tiny beading. The Towle collection can be worn, as well as used on your Christmas tree. Designer: Ted Merry. Dimensions: 3" h × 2¼" w. Issue price: $10.00.

"Three French Hens"
(third edition—third day)

The third day of Christmas medallion is "weighted," (as are all ornaments in this collection), triangular in shape, and depicts, as I am sure you have guessed, "Three French Hens," with delicate scrolling on one side and a Christmas Rose on the other. It recalls the legend of a little shepherd girl who followed the gift-bearing shepherds to the manger in Bethlehem with a sad heart, for she had no gift for the newborn King. Suddenly an angel appeared in her path scattering beautiful white roses. The little girl gathered some of the blossoms and laid them around the crib in the manger. These flowers had never been seen before and came to be known as the "Christmas Rose," according to the legend. Designer: Ted Merry. Dimensions: 2¾" h × 2¼" w. Issue price: $10.00.

17

"Four Calling Birds"
(fourth edition—fourth day)

"Calling Birds, Four of Them" are the attraction of the fourth medallion in this series, issued in 1974, keeping the tradition of the song. The other side of this ornament depicts the birth of Christ. A "trilogy" of stars is depicted. The stars came so close together on that night so long ago and their brilliance was so great that they appeared as one star. That star is now known as the Star of Bethlehem, the star that guided the three wise men, shepherds, and others to the birthplace of the newborn baby, Jesus Christ. Designer: Ted Merry. Dimensions: 3″ h × 2¼″ w. Issue price: $15.00.

"Five Golden Rings"
(fifth edition—fifth day)

Towle was inspired in 1975 to produce two ornaments commemorating the "Fifth Day of Christmas," one in all-sterling and the other introducing a combination of sterling and vermeil or gold. This ornament is oval-shaped, with beading and a sun-burst type design surrounding a smooth-surfaced plate showing "raised" "Five Golden Rings" encircled over a cross. The other side was inspired by the frosted windows of an ancient cathedral in France, with scrollwork surrounding the windows, reminiscent of the arches and columns of that cathedral. The issue price of the sterling, combined with vermeil, was slightly more than the all-sterling and is also becoming hard to find and expensive. Designer: Ted Merry. Dimensions: 2¾″ h × 2¼″ w. Issue price: $15.00.

"Six Geese A-Laying"
(sixth edition—sixth day)

The celebration of the bicentennial was considered in the design of the "Sixth Day of Christmas" ornament. A circle of holly leaves and balls frames our symbolic Liberty Bell, commemorating our country's two-hundredth birthday. The other side features "Six Geese A-Laying." This ornament is a beautiful bicen-

Towle's 1972   Second Edition "Two Turtle Doves"
PHOTO BY TOWLE

Towle's 1973—Third Edition   "Three French Hens"
PHOTO BY TOWLE

Towle's 1974   Fourth Edition   "Four Calling Birds"
PHOTO BY TOWLE

Tree Topping

Gorham tops off their collections with a tree topping for your collection and tree. It is a sterling cross with a sunburst design at the top. A fitting way to top your sterling tree. Designer: J. Russell Price, past director of design. Dimension: 7¼″ h. Issue price: $16.50.

Gorham's "Rocking Horse"   *1979*
PHOTO BY GORHAM

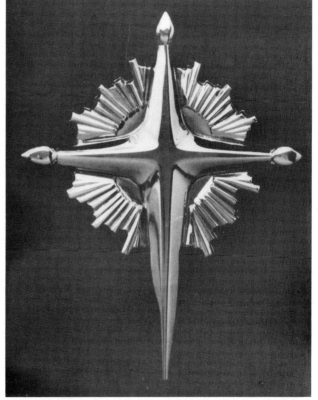

Gorham's "Steam Engine"   *1979*
PHOTO BY GORHAM

Gorham's Tree Topper—Sunburst Cross
PHOTO BY GORHAM

___ 2 ___
The Towle Silversmiths Collections

The Twelve Days of Christmas
and
Christmas Melodies Medallions

The Towle Manufacturing Company, known for fine silver craftsmanship since 1690, has immortalized a favorite Christmas carol, "The Twelve Days of Christmas," with a sterling-silver, medallion ornament collection. Starting in 1971, the company has issued and anticipates continuing to issue the twelve days of Christmas, keeping in the tradition of the song, one ornament issued each year, completing the set by 1982. Each ornament is copywrited, dated, and beautifully designed (1972–1978) by Ted Merry, a member of the silversmiths' staff at Towle. After each year's production is completed, the dies are destroyed or retired, never to be used again.

The method for making these medallions is by the direct reverse cutting in steel of the striking die by hand. The cutting of this die is done by the designer/craftsman himself who searches the final solution in process.

Towle's Twelve Days Medallions have proven to be one of the favorites of collectors.

Towle's second collection called "Christmas Melodies Medallions" started in 1978 depicting Christmas carols. The first issue is "Silent Night, Holy Night."

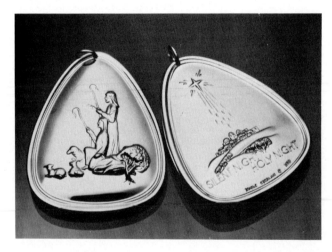

Towle's 1978 First Edition "*Christmas Melodies*"
PHOTO BY TOWLE

"The Twelve Days of Christmas"

"Partridge in a Pear Tree"
(first edition—first day)

"A Partridge in a Pear Tree", the first edition issued in 1971 at $10.00 is being sold at the time of this writing for as much as $650.00, if you can find it. This disc-shaped ornament is actually two discs fused together with hammered finished edges. On one side is a "raised" designed pear tree with a partridge perched on a branch. A

"A Partridge" 1972
(first day)

Catching the spirit of the "Twelve Days of Christmas," International issued a "Partridge in a Pear Tree" in 1972. The ornament is approximately eight inches long, open cut on the side to show the red enameling inside. An oval, sterling, black-coated, embossed disc is attached on the back and front. The prominent areas of the discs are polished to bring out the designs of "pears and a partridge in a tree." It, as all in this collection, is marked, "International—Sterling."

"Two Turtle Doves"
(second day)

The inside of the second day is green and the raised areas of the black-coated discs are polished to bring out "two loving Turtle Doves, perched on a branch, framed with hearts."

"Three French Hens"
(third day)

Three nesting French hens, one over the other, are surrounded by holly leaves and berries and are depicted on the black-coated sterling disc of the "third day" ornament with blue-enameling interior.

"Four Calling Birds"
(fourth day)

Red enameling is on the inside and "Four Calling Birds" are on the outside of the fourth ornament. The "Birds" are perched in a delicate hanging cage with a leaf design at the bottom and a perky bow is tied at the top, on the black-coated discs.

"Five Golden Rings"
(fifth day)

An exhausted-looking, kneeling knight or knave holds a pillow with his offering of "Five Golden Rings," and a touch of holly is the center of attention on the "fifth." Red is the "inside" color.

Partridge in a Pear Tree
PHOTO BY KEVIN NASH

Two Turtle Doves
PHOTO BY KEVIN NASH

Three French Hens
PHOTO BY KEVIN NASH

Four Calling Birds
PHOTO BY KEVIN NASH

Five Golden Rings
PHOTO BY KEVIN NASH

"Six Geese A-Laying"
(sixth day)

Green on the inside and six long neck, proud geese on the outside, a-laying silver eggs (three can be seen).

"Seven Swans A-Swimming"
(seventh day)

One majestic swan is A-Swimming along, representing herself and six others (not seen) on a holly pond. The interior is blue.

"Eight Maids A-Milking"
(eighth day)

A beautiful Dutch maid, wearing the traditional "wooden shoes," delicately designed apron and a "bar" over her shoulders with a milk pail on each end. The smiling Dutch lass is profusely surrounded in holly; red is the color showing through the side openings.

"Nine Ladies Dancing"
(ninth day)

You get the impression that eight other ladies may be in a chorus line dancing behind the one shown on the "ninth day" disc; holly and berries frame the figure; red enameling is used on the inside.

"Ten Lords A-Leaping"
(tenth day)

Green is on the inside and one lord leaping over holly is on the outside of the "tenth day." Dressed in the manner of a "long ago, English lord," he is leaping ahead of nine others.

"Eleven Pipers Piping"
(eleventh day)

This piper piping is leading a pack of eleven, making holiday music. All decked out in a darling outfit, he with the rest of his band, could "stir a lot of mice" on Christmas Eve.

Six Geese-A-Laying
PHOTO BY KEVIN NASH

Seven Swans-A-Swimming
PHOTO BY KEVIN NASH

Eight Maids-A-Milking
PHOTO BY KEVIN NASH

Nine Ladies Dancing
PHOTO BY KEVIN NASH

Ten Lords-A-Leaping
PHOTO BY KEVIN NASH

Eleven Pipers Piping
PHOTO BY KEVIN NASH

"Twelve Drummers Drumming"
(twelfth day)

Epaulets on his shoulders and sticks in his hand, this drummer drumming is the leader of the band, the band of twelve drummers representing the "twelfth day" of Christmas—and "a Partridge in a Pear Tree!"

This collection was designed by Carl Sundberg, free-lance artist, in conjunction with Phil De-Nino, former Director of International's Design Department.

Twelve Drummers Drumming
PHOTO BY KEVIN NASH

Santas
(Silver-plated–Limited–Issue price: $5.00 each)

One of the most beloved figures the world over is "Santa Claus," "Kris Kringle," "Father Christmas," "The Yule Man," "Le Petit Noel," "Chriskindl," "St. Nicholas," or "Grandfather Frost"—in Italy there is a female Santa called "Befana" and in Russia her counterpart is "Babouchka." Wherever, Santa is a unique, colorful personality in his "uniform," wearing a red suit trimmed in white ermine, with long, flowing white beard and hair. He is characterized by his rosy, ruddy cheeks, twinkling eyes, and "round belly that shakes like jelly" and of course his familiar, famous Ho! Ho! Ho!

"Santa"
(first edition 1972)

Stuart A. Young, designer at International, has captured in silver the many busy moments of Santa at Christmas, starting with a gnomelike figure of Santa in the 1972 first edition of this collection. Instead of flopping, his cap stands straight up as if his head were cone-shaped. His face and beard are finely detailed and his belly dwarfs the balance of his body. The back is dated "Christmas 1972" and hallmarked. For this and each subsequent year, a gold-plated version was also produced. Dimensions: 3½" l × 1½" w.

The 1978 Insilco Collection
PHOTO BY INSILCO

International's complete set of the "12 Days of Christmas,"
shown in their specially designed case.
PHOTO BY INSILCO

International's First Edition "Santa"   *1972*
PHOTO BY INSILCO

International's Third Edition "Santa"   *1974*
PHOTO BY INSILCO

"Santa"
(second edition 1973)

Santa's cap is conventionally "flopped" in 1973. He carries his bag of gifts, his head decreased since 1972, and his legs are seen, boots and all. His belly is still pronounced and so are his smiling face and lovable beard. Santa is beautiful both coming and going. He is as articulately designed on the back as the front. His belt and boot on the back show the date and hallmark. Dimensions: 2½″ h × 1½″ w.

"Santa"
(third edition 1974)

Making his rounds, Santa is caught climbing down the chimney in 1974. "Not a creature is stirring" and the fire in the hearth has subsided because icicles have formed on the chimney top. Santa has his bag on his back and a smile on his face. On the reverse side, you know someone will be delighted to find the little sailboat in Santa's bag, under the tree. The chimney is dated 1974 and hall-marked. Dimensions: 2⅝″ h × 1⅜″ w.

"Santa"
(fourth edition 1975)

Santa, sitting in his sleigh, 1975, looks as if he were posing to be photographed. He is delivering another sailboat and a horn. Sleigh bells are shown down the front of the sleigh and the date is on the back. Dimensions: 2⅝″ h × 1½″ w.

27

"Santa"
(fifth edition 1976)

Beating a bicentennial drum in '76, Santa took time out and joined the celebration of our two-hundredth birthday with a light drum roll.

He has the same smile and beard, but his belly is hidden by his bicentennial drum decorated with stars and "76." He is dated again and hallmarked on the back. Dimensions: 2¾" h × 1½" w.

"Santa"
(sixth edition 1977)

It's not quite Christmas yet and Santa checks his "North Pole" mailbox in 1977 to find it is filled with more orders to deliver on the "Night before Christmas." He has been by the toy shop though, because the bag on the ground near his foot is brimming with toys. Dimensions: 2⁶/₈" h × 1½" w.

"Santa"
(seventh edition 1978)

Santa made his rounds in 1978 and will continue to in future years, as planned by International, in both silver plate and gold plate, and I am counting on Stuart A. Young to candidly catch him in the act as he did in 1978, "Standing in His Booth." Dimensions: 2¾" h × 1¾" w.

This collection is annual and limited. The dies are destroyed after production, never to be used again.

Photo Cube/Wooden Stand 1975 only

International's designer, Joseph A. Chalifoux, created an ornament to grace the tree, table, or desk called the "Photo Cube Ornament" in 1975. The four-sided ornament holds four photographs of loved ones or friends. It is square-shaped in the center area and tapers gradually to the top and bottom in a lantern manner. It is six inches long. The black wooden stand has a silver-plated wire, arched from its base, from which the "Cube" hangs. Issue price: $15.00.

International's Fourth Edition "Santa"   1975
PHOTO BY INSILCO

International's Fifth Edition "Santa"   1976
PHOTO BY INSILCO

International's Photo Cube   1974
PHOTO BY INSILCO

International's Sixth Edition "Santa"   1977
PHOTO BY INSILCO

International's First Day of Christmas Pendant   1974
PHOTO BY INSILCO

International's Seventh Edition "Santa"   1978
This is the Last Edition.
PHOTO BY INSILCO

"Twelve Days of Christmas Pendants"

The center-designed sterling "Discs" used on the "Twelve Days of Christmas Ornaments," were issued by International to be used as jewelry and/or Christmas ornaments. This collection of twelve is an interpretation of each of the "Twelve Days of Christmas." Dimensions: 2¼" l × 1½" h. Issue price: $10.00 each.

Christmas Rose 1976 (Pendant/Ornament)

The "Christmas Rose," with its many legends and special holiday meanings, was beautifully designed by Stuart A. Young and issued by International in a 2¼" sterling pendant/ornament in 1976. Issue price: $5.00.

Coach Lantern 1973

Reminiscent of the days of yore is the "Coach Lantern" ornament, issued in silver plate in 1973.
   Joseph A. Chalifoux, designer, created a realistic "Coach Lantern" ornament for the tree right down to the last detail, with a red candle, wick and all, in the center of the square, open-sided 4" ornament, tapering to the top. Issue price: $15.00.

Twin Angel Tree Topping 1977

A silver-plated "Twin Angel Tree Topping" made its way from designer Stuart A. Young's drawing board into homes in 1977 to reside at the top of the Christmas tree. The "Twin Angels" are winged, haloed, convexed, and connected, and are designed in a contemporary fashion, and I might add, beautiful! They are no longer made, and I'm looking for one! Dimension: 5" h. Issue price: $15.00.

Angel Bell Ornament

Beverly Chase (the only female designer of ornaments to date at International) has to her credit a gorgeous gold- and silver-plated "Angel Bell Ornament," issued in 1977. The face of the ornament is angelic, as one would guess, her

International's Christmas Rose
PHOTO BY INSILCO

International's Lantern Ornament
PHOTO BY INSILCO

hands are clasped in front as if she were praying and her sleeves fall in drapes and folds. She is gold-plated from the waistline up, including her spread wings and halo. The silver-plated skirt forms the bell. This duel-purposed ornament can be used to call the family to the holiday dinner table or decorate the "Tannenbaum." International has not decided at this writing whether she will be issued again. Dimension: 4½"h. Issue price: $10.95.

Snowflake Ornament/Medallion 1977

A delicate, small, lacey "Snowflake," designed in sterling by Edward S. Buchko, was made available for the 1977 Christmas tree or jewelry gift giving. It is a welcome addition in that no two "Snowflakes" issued to date by any manufacturer are alike, just as those "falling from the sky." Dimension: 1¾" h. Issue price: $15.00.

International's Twin Angel Tree Top   *1974*
PHOTO BY INSILCO

International's Snowflake
PHOTO BY KEVIN NASH

International's Angel Bell Ornament   *1975*

Stained Glass Collection

"Toy Soldier" 1978

Decked out in all his regalia, on guard and at attention, is this "Toy Soldier." He is standing in the arched doorway of this scrolled, silver-plated, stained-glass-type ornament to make sure that no one got a peek at the gifts under the tree until Christmas morn, in 1978. Background color—red. Designer: Ronald Goudace. Dimensions: 3½″ h × 1⅞″ w. Issue price: $8.00.

"Angel" 1978

A stained-glass, lacey, silver-plated "Angel" from International joined the host of angels on my tree in 1978. Her body is bordered in a silver plate with ornate plate scrolling. Her wings, head, and halo are all plated. Background color—blue. Designer: Stuart A. Young. Dimensions: 3³/₁₆″ h × 2¼″ w. Issue price: $8.00.

"Joy" 1978

A round, scrolled disc with "Joy" boldly designed across the center, created in silver plate over a green, stained-glass background is one of International's 1978 offerings. This ornament very simply conveys the feeling of the spirit of Christmas. Designer: Ronald Goodes. Dimensions: 2⅞″ diameter. Issue price: $8.00.

"Christmas Tree" 1978

In 1978 from International came a stained-glass "Christmas Tree." This ornament is shaped like a tree, outlined in silver plate, with branch effects and decorated all over with ornate silver plate. Background color is green. Designer: Stuart A. Young. Dimensions: 3⁷/₁₆″ h × 3¼″ w. Issue price: $8.00.

"Snowflake" 1978

A boldly designed, open-worked, contemporary, silver-plated "Snowflake," over blue stained glass is a part of International's 1978 collection of seven ornaments. Designer: Carl Aichler. Dimension: 2⅞″ in diameter.
Issue price: $8.00.

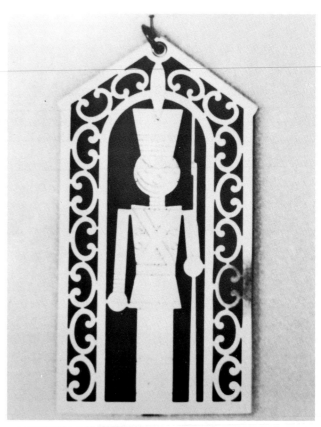

International's Stained Glass "Toy Soldier"   *1978*
PHOTO BY INSILCO

International's Stained Glass "Angel"   *1978*
PHOTO BY INSILCO

International's Stained Glass X-mas Tree   *1978*
PHOTO BY INSILCO

International's Stained Glass "Joy"   *1978*
PHOTO BY INSILCO

International's Stained Glass "Snowflake"   *1978*
PHOTO BY INSILCO

"Bell" 1978

To ring in the holiday season for 1978, a "Bell" was created by International, but don't try to ring it even if it does have a clapper. It is a flat Christmas ornament in the shape of a bell, with lacey-designed silver plate over red stained glass. Designer: Stuart A. Young. Dimensions: 2⅞" h × 3⅛" w. Issue price: $8.00.

"Dove of Peace" 1978

To finish off their 1978 holiday collection and to convey their wishes to all for the coming new year, International issued a "Dove of Peace" ornament. The oblong-shaped ornament is outlined in silver plate, and an intricately designed dove is a-lighting above the word "Peace" that is boldly designed across the bottom. Background color is stained-glass blue. Designer: Ronald Goudace. Dimensions: 3½" w × 1⅞" h. Issue price: $8.00.

American Archives Collection

A few years ago, a new division, headed by Ashton Edwards, was created at the International Silver Company, called "American Archives." This basically, a catalog sales division in a direct-catalog-mail program, makes some of their products not sold through stores available to private individuals in their homes. Many of Insilco's collectable products sold through stores and collectable products made by other companies, such as Royal Worcester, Royal Daulton, Kaiser, Ambassador Luggage, Columbia Records and Tapes, Spode China, Royal Crown Derby, Leyendecker, Beswicks and others are sold through International's "American Archives" catalog.

In 1977, Christmas ornaments were created by the company for this division.

International's Stained Glass "Bell"   *1978*
PHOTO BY INSILCO

International's Stained Glass "Dove of Peace"   1978
PHOTO BY INSILCO

"Cherub"
(1976—first edition)

A "Cherub" with a harp, in silver plate, to be used as a tree ornament or pendant was made available through the American Archives Catalog. Dimension: 2½″ h. Issue price: $7.50.

"Cherub"
(1977—second edition)

The 1977, silver-plated "Cherub" with a horn was issued as a part of a continuing series by the American Archives Division through their holiday catalog. Dimension: 2½″ h. Issue price: $8.50.

"Christmas Tree" 1977

A Christmas tree ornament in a stamped-out, lacey design, with a miniature bell at its base was created in silver plate and sold in 1977 through the American Archives Catalog. Dimension: 2¾″. Issue price: $6.50.

International's Cherub   First Edition   1976
PHOTO BY INSILCO

35

International's Christmas Tree   1977
PHOTO BY KEVIN NASH

International's Cherub   *Second Edition*   1977
PHOTO BY INSILCO

Collection of Four Ornaments 1978

In 1978, "a touch of glass, a touch of color," seems to have been uppermost in many of the Christmas ornament designers' minds, as evidenced by the many sterling and plated ornaments issued with "color" that year.

The "American Archives" division of International became a leader in the "color" area with their creative designers, Ronald and Frank Goudace. Ronald was a key person in assisting me at this division, along with Ms. Smart and the division head, Ashton (Ash) Edwards. Thanks to all of them for the following information.

Each ornament in this collection was designed in two ways:

1) "Double" or "Stained Glass," with color glass between two of the same stamped-out ornaments in silver plate, each issued at $8.00.

2) "Single" stamping of the ornament and no color or glass, each issued at $5.00.

"Kneeling Angel"

The "Kneeling Angel" for 1978 is 3⅜" h and the color of the glass is blue. Her halo is a ring of stars, and the color can be seen through the design of her wing, the back, sleeve, and the bottom of her gown. Designer: Ronald Goudace.

"Hexagon Snowflake"

From point to point the "Hexagon Snowflake" is 3⅜". It is modernistic in design and the color showing through is blue. Designer: Frank Goudace. creation.

International's Angel   *1978*

International's Hexagon Snowflake   *1978*

"Noel"

"Holly and Berries"

A clever combination of using highly polished brass, silver plate, and red glass was used in the creation of "Noel" in 1978. The silver-plated, grille-type stamping designed round ornament has red, peeking through the grillwork at the top and bottom, with "Noel" emblazened boldly in brass "script" acros the center. A striking beauty! Designer: Ronald Goudace.

Seven clusters of berries and five leaves are the ovaled-center attention of the "Holly and Berries" ornament with green glass showing through in 1978. Designer: Ronald Goudace. Dimension: $3\,5/16''$ h.

—— 4 ——
The Wallace Silversmiths' Collections

The Annual Wallace Christmas Bells (Silver-plated)
The Annual Wallace Peace Doves (Sterling/Vermeil-Vermeil)
The Wallace Open Bell

The Wallace Silversmith Company was founded by Robert Wallace and Samuel Simpson on May 1, 1855, and was purchased by the Hamilton Watch Company in 1959. Wallace manufactures all types of holloware, flatware, and stainless steel. Nineteen seventy-one marked the beginning of a new line of special creations, annual Christmas ornaments, from the artisans of Wallace staff with their offering of the first annual Christmas Bell and the first annual Peace Dove.

The Annual Christmas Bells

"Christmas Bell"
(first edition 1971)

After over one hundred years of manufacturing fine hollow and flatware for the home and institution, Wallace created a "Christmas Tree Ornament" in 1971, marking the first issue of the annual "Christmas Bell." The silver-plated round bell grows more meaningful, expensive, and elusive (to the collector) each year. At this writing it is one of the three "most rare" ornaments made and your "Bell" collection is incomplete without it. The design of the 1971 "Christmas Bell" is holly leaves and berries

Wallace Silver Co. 1971 First Edition Sleigh Bell PHOTO BY WALLACE

around the center, hallmarked and dated at the
bottom. This bell ornament will never be repeated again for sale after the 1971 holiday
season and to secure it you must be willing to pay
whatever the seller asks from a secondary
market. Dimensions: 2¾″ × 2½″ each. Issue
price: $12.95.

"Christmas Bell"
(second edition 1972)

Santa, in his sleigh loaded with gifts, and his eight
tiny reindeer are circling the center of the second "Christmas Bell" in 1972. Each year the bell
is issued in silver-plate, hallmarked and dated
and never repeated. Issue price: $12.95.

"Christmas Bell"
(third edition 1973)

The 1973 "Christmas Bell" wishes all a "Merry
Christmas-1973" around the center, with a little
holly thrown in, dated and hallmarked on the
bottom. Issue price: $12.95.

*Wallace Silver Co. 1972 Second Edition
Sleigh Bell* PHOTO BY WALLACE

*Wallace Silver Co. 1973 Third Edition
Sleigh Bell* PHOTO BY WALLACE

"Christmas Bell"
(fourth edition 1974)

Children's toys is the theme of the fourth "Bell" issued in 1974. A horn, a jack-in-the-box, a gingerbread man, an old-fashioned train engine with coal car and passenger car connected, a doll, a drum, a rocking horse, a spinning top, a tree, and a horn are all molded around the center. The date and hallmark are on the bottom. Issue price: $12.95.

"Christmas Bell"
(fifth edition 1975)

Elflike children, hand in hand playing "Ring Around" with 1975, are the center circle of design on this year's dated, hallmarked offering. Issue price: $13.50.

"Christmas Bell"
(sixth edition 1976)

A beautiful bicentennial motif of our national eagle, liberty bell and the dates 1776-1976 is entwined with Christmas holly and berries and "Commemorates the Heritage of Freedom and Faith where the Joys of Christmas may be shared by all." The 1976 bell is a rare edition of this collection in that it was also collected by the bicentennial collectors. Issue price: $13.95.

"Christmas Bell"
(seventh edition 1977)

Christmas greenery, peace doves in flight, and the date 1977 encircles the annual, dated, and hallmarked ornament. Issue price: $14.95.

"Christmas Bell"
(eighth edition 1978)

The eighth annual "Christmas Bell" is center circled with Christmas roses and the issue year, 1978. This edition, like those before and those to come, is silver-plated, hallmarked, dated, and will never be repeated, assuring collectors of a lifetime treasure to recall happy holiday seasons of the past. Issue price: $14.95.

Wallace Silver Co. 1974 Fourth Edition Sleigh Bell PHOTO BY WALLACE

Wallace Silver Co. 1975 Fifth Edition Sleigh Bell PHOTO BY WALLACE

Wallace Silver Co. 1976 Sixth Edition Sleigh Bell PHOTO BY WALLACE

Wallace Silver Co. 1978 Eighth Edition Sleigh Bell PHOTO BY WALLACE

The Wallace Silversmith Company plans to continue this series that will grow in meaning and value.

"Christmas Bell"
(ninth edition — 1979)

A lovely village snow scene, poinsettia garland and the mark "1979" circle the ninth annual edition of Wallace's limited-edition 1979 "Christmas Bell." Issue price: $15.95.

Wallace Silver Co. 1977 Seventh Edition Sleigh Bell PHOTO BY WALLACE

41

The Annual Peace Doves (Sterling)

The "Peace Dove" symbolizes peace, innocence, gentleness, and the Holy Ghost, according to the Random House Dictionary. Wallace created and issued the first of the annual "Peace Dove" Christmas ornament/medallions in 1971, exemplifying peace and love for the Christmas season. The doves have been created in various designs and offered in all-sterling, all-gold (plated over sterling), and a combination of sterling ring with all-gold-plated dove.

"Peace Dove"
(first edition 1971)

The first edition of the "Peace Dove" annual ornament was offered by Wallace in 1971. This dull-finished, all-sterling ornament is a beautifully crafted design of four "Peace Doves" with their spread wings connecting, forming a square in a cut-out manner. Their beaks and feathers are finely etched. In the circle of a blue enamel ring on the reverse side is engraved, "Peace on Earth" and "1971," creating a lasting treasure to mark the personal memories of that year. Each year the ornament will be hallmarked and dated but never again repeated. Dimensions: 2¾" × 2⅜". Sterling only—dull finish. Issue price: $11.95.

"Peace Dove"
(second edition 1972)

Two "Peace Doves" flying through an oval ring in dull-finish sterling is the second issue of this collection, offered in 1972. One "Dove's" finely etched breast and spread wing is shown facing the viewer; the other's back is seen. The back of this ornament has blue enamel on each side of the ring, with "Peace on Earth" on one and 1972 on the other side of the ring. Dimensions: 2¾" × 2". Sterling only—dull finish. Issue price: $12.95.

Wallace Silver Co. 1971 First Edition Peace Dove PHOTO BY WALLACE

Wallace Silver Co. 1972 Second Edition
Peace Dove PHOTO BY WALLACE

"Peace Dove"
(third edition 1973)

The third in this series, offered in 1973, is a circle (ring) with two "Doves" kissing (their beaks are meeting), and their wings spread upward as if they were alighting. A blue-enamel circle on the back is engraved with "Peace on Earth—1973—Good Will toward Men." The beauty of this collection is the importance of the etching of the Doves, both back and front. Blue enamel seems to make its last appearance with this ornament. For the first time, in 1973, an issue was also made in gold plate. Dimensions: 2⅝″ × 2¼″. Issue prices: sterling, $13.95; 18 kt. goldplate, $23.50.

"Peace Dove"
(fourth edition 1974)

A single "dove," with very finely detailed feathers, flying upwards at an angle, presented in a highly polished oval, is the 1974 edition of this collection. In raised letters on the back is Wallace's message of "Peace on Earth 1974, Good Will Toward Men." The gold-plated issue made its second debut in 1974. Dimensions: 3¼″ × 1¾″. Issue prices: sterling, $17.50; 18 kt. goldplate, $22.50.

"Peace Dove"
(fifth edition 1975)

A "ring-encircled," single, soaring "Dove" bearing the annual message "Peace on Earth 1975, Good Will toward Men" on the back is that year's holiday issue. The 1975 ornament was issued in three variations: one—all-sterling; two—all-gold; and three—a gold "Dove" in the silver ring. Dimensions: 2⅝″ × 2⅜″. Issue prices: sterling $17.50; 18 kt. gold plate, $25.00; 24 kt. gold-plated Dove/sterling ring, $25.00.

"Peace Dove"
(sixth edition 1976)

The 1976 ornament was issued in three variations: all-sterling, all-gold-plated, and gold-plated "Dove" in silver circle. The oval ring has two "Doves" soaring in flight, one higher than the other, both facing the viewer. "Peace on Earth 1976, Good Will toward Men" is the message on the reverse side. Dimensions: 2½" × 1⅝". Issue prices: sterling, $19.95; 24 kt. gold-plated "Dove"/sterling ring, $27.50; 18 kt. gold plate, $27.50.

"Peace Dove"
(seventh edition 1977)

Smaller in price and in size, a single "Dove" in a pear-shaped ring, with the annual holiday greeting of "Peace on Earth 1977, Good Will toward Men" on the back was issued in both all-sterling and all-gold-plated for 1977. Dimensions: 2¼" × 1⅜". Issue prices: sterling, $15.95; 24 kt. gold-plated/sterling ring, $16.95.

"Peace Dove"
(eighth edition 1978)

Two encircled graceful "Doves" flew into the holiday season bearing tidings. On the back is "Peace on Earth 1978, Good Will toward Men" from the Wallace Silversmith Co., in all-sterling only. It is interesting to me how the designers can change the shape and the position of the Doves to make them different and special each year. No ornament in this collection will ever be repeated. Dimensions: 2⅝" × 2⅜". Issue price: sterling, $16.95. Collection closed.

Wallace Silver Co. 1973 Third Edition
Peace Dove PHOTO BY WALLACE

Wallace Silver Co. 1974 Fourth Edition
Peace Dove   PHOTO BY WALLACE

Wallace Silver Co. 1975 Fifth Edition
Peace Dove   PHOTO BY WALLACE

45

Wallace Silver Co. 1976 Sixth Edition
Peace Dove   PHOTO BY WALLACE

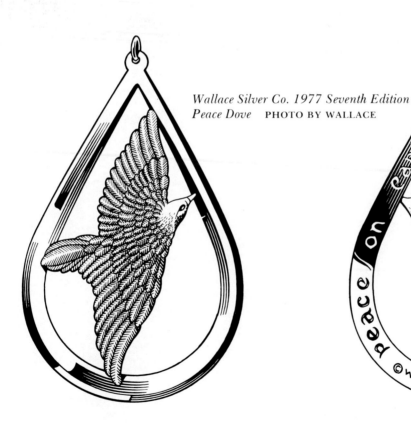

Wallace Silver Co. 1977 Seventh Edition
Peace Dove   PHOTO BY WALLACE

Wallace Silver Co. 1978 Eighth Edition
Peace Dove 1978–this is the final Peace Dove.
collection closed.

The Open Bell Collection
Holly–Poinsettias–Snowflake

Wallace Open Bells. RIGHT TO LEFT: *"Holly",*
"Poinsettia", "Snowflake" PHOTO BY WALLACE

Two "Open Bells" in silver plate were made by Wallace in 1973, one with "Enameled Holly" on the top and the other with "Enameled Poinsettias".

The 1978 offering of this bell has a multi-faceted "Snowflake" in multi-color enameling.

This collection is not annual and repeated, but they are beautiful and "spark up" the holiday tree. These bells can be engraved to commemorate the year of purchase. Dimensions: 3″ × 2½″ each. Issue prices: 1973, Holly, $12.95; Poinsettia, $12.95; 1978, Snowflake, $14.95.

5

The Reed and Barton Collections

In Taunton, Massachusetts, 1824, Isaac Babbitt and William W. Crossman formed a company that led to what is now known as Reed & Barton.

It has become the most prolific in Christmas ornament collections. Starting in 1971 they have presented to date:

Christmas Cross collection
Christmas Stars
Holly Ball collection
Snowflakes collection
The "Trim-a-Tree Picture Frame" collection, gift-boxed singly and in pairs
The "Tree Castle" collection in vermeil
The "Twelve Days of Christmas Bells" collection, issued two-by-two, beginning with the Partridge and the Turtle Dove

Christmas Cross Collection

The 1971 "Christmas Cross"

Reed & Barton's first limited-edition, 1971 "Christmas Cross" is a richly detailed sterling or vermeil authentic reproduction of a fourteenth-century design by Gallicus, a renowned artist of Prague, a European culture center of that era. This collection is of historical interest, as you will find in each year's issue. The dies are destroyed after each year's production run, assuring the owner of a collector's item. Designer: Gretta Roberts. Dimensions: 3⅜″ h × 3⅜″ w. Issue prices: sterling, $10.00; vermeil, $17.50.

The 1972 "Christmas Cross"

My favorite, to date, is the 1972 "Christmas Cross." It is a jewel-like modified quatrcfoil, an authentic reproduction of an antique processional cross from the Byzantine period of the sixth century.

Plaudits are extended to the researchers, historians, and craftsmen at Reed & Barton. Designer: Clark Lofgren. Dimensions: 3⅜″ h × 3⅜″ w. Issue prices: sterling, $10.00; vermeil, $17.50.

The 1973 "Christmas Cross"

Inspiration for the 1973 "Christmas Cross" came from art forms of the Middle Ages. The Cross is a stylized reproduction of the medieval Cross of the West Gable of England's renowned Washburn church in Worcestershire. The 1973 Reed & Barton "Christmas Cross" is the first ornament I purchased which gave birth to my collections, resulting in this book. I suppose I will have to retract an earlier statement and say this is my favorite! Designer: Gretta Roberts. Dimensions: 3¾″ h × 3¼″ w. Issue prices: sterling, $10.00; vermeil, $17.50.

The 1974 "Christmas Cross"

An elegant ancient cross at the top of Funchal cathedral in the city of Madeira is reproduced on the 1974 "Christmas Cross." The women flower sellers of Madeira remove their huge baskets of flowers at the steps of the famous cathedral before entering to pray, so that by nightfall, their baskets will be empty. Designer: Gretta Roberts. Dimensions: 3¼″ h × 3¼″ w. Issue prices: sterling, $12.95; vermeil, $20.00.

The 1975 "Christmas Cross"

The historic Patonce Patee Cross, in French Medieval Heraldry, symbolized chivalric honor, valor, and sacrifice and adorned the helmets and escutcheons of the Norman Knights during the crusades of the eleventh and twelfth centuries. The 1975 offering is the Patonce Patee Cross, produced by Reed & Barton. Designer: Clark Lofgren. Dimensions: 2¾″ h × 2¾″ w. Issue prices: sterling, $12.95; vermeil, $20.00.

The 1976 "Christmas Cross"

The 1976 "Christmas Cross" is a reproduction of the Gothic, hand-carved architectural rosette that adorns the great cathedral of Chester, in England. The cathedral, built by Kings Henry VII and VIII in the fifteenth and sixteenth centuries, is an example of the supreme English church woodwork. Designer: Clark Lofgren. Dimensions: 3″ h ×3″ w. Issue prices: sterling, $13.95; vermeil, $19.95.

The 1977 "Christmas Cross"

An eight-pointed cross, worn by the eleventh century religious order of Chivalry called the "Knight Hospitalers," was reproduced and issued in 1977 by Reed & Barton. The "Knights Hospitalers," later called the "Order of the Malt," was founded in 1070 A.D. and was comprised of knights of noble descent who in the twelfth century provided hospital service to the needy during the European crusades. The raised spiral ornaments on the 1977 cross were inspired by the ancient Neolithic stone carvings from the

The Reed and Barton 1971 First Edition Christmas Cross
PHOTO BY REED AND BARTON

The 1972 Second Annual Christmas Cross in Sterling and Vermeil by Reed and Barton
PHOTO BY REED AND BARTON

The 1973 Third Annual Christmas Cross by Reed and Barton
PHOTO BY REED AND BARTON

The 1974 Fourth Annual Reed and Barton Cross
PHOTO BY REED AND BARTON

Temple of Hal Tarxian on the island of Malta. Designer: George Pinhero. Dimensions: 2½″ h × 2½″ w. Issue prices: sterling, $15.00; vermeil, $18.50.

The 1978 "Christmas Cross"

This is the eighth in a distinguished series of annual "Christmas Crosses" in richly detailed sterling silver by Reed & Barton. The 1978 "Christmas Cross" design is from a celebrated twelfth-century Swedish mural now in a private European collection. The rich mosaic of silvery acanthus leaves adorning a clean linear cross is one of the finest extant examples of Scandinavian-Romanesque art.

Following the demise of Roman political supremacy in the fourth century, a new Early Christian and Byzantine art style evolved which eventually became known as "Romanesque." The resulting spread of Christianity brought the finest of these Romanesque elements of ancient Mediterranean art to Northern Europe, where it developed its own distinctive Scandinavian style.

This richly detailed, sterling silver original—a Limited Edition—is a charming decorative piece to enhance your yule tree. At the conclusion of the 1978 production run, the dies used to manufacture this cross were destroyed, thus assuring the owner of a valued collector's item. With every passing year, each authentic new edition will make the Reed & Barton Christmas Cross collection ever more personal, versatile, and unique. Designer: Clark Lofgren. Issue prices: sterling, $16.00; vermeil, $20.00.

The 1979 "Christmas Cross"

This ninth annual sterling silver cross, steeped in historcal tradition, was inspired by a 14th Century decorative encaustic tile that came from a cathedral altar in Northern England. The word "encaustic" (meaning "Burnt-in") is Greek in derivation and refers to an ancient method of painting with hot wax, which was developed to protect Greek statues from the elements. The Romans and Egyptians advanced this technique to such durability that it became an artistic form of expression, as well as surface protection for painting. The English encaustic tile used in the design for this year's cross is one of the few remaining examples of this ancient art form and is now in a private collection. Although the dies for this limited-edition ornament have been de-

The 1975 Fifth Annual Reed and Barton Cross
PHOTO BY REED AND BARTON

The 1976 Sixth Annual Reed and Barton Cross
PHOTO BY REED AND BARTON

The 1977 Seventh Annual Reed and Barton Cross
PHOTO BY REED AND BARTON

The 1978 Eighth Annual Reed and Barton Cross
PHOTO BY REED AND BARTON

stroyed, the ancient encaustic art form is permanently captured in the 1979 Cross. Designer: Todd C. Scott. Dimensions: 2¾″ × 2¾″. Issue prices: sterling, $20.00; vermeil, $24.00.

Christmas Stars
(Annual Limited Editions)

The legend of the "Christmas Star" has been both inspiring and haunting to mankind. Three scientific theories are that the brilliant light was caused by Halley's Comet, by the converging of the three planets, Mars, Saturn and Jupiter (an occurrence in every eight-hundred years), or, as still others believe, by the appearance of a new temporary star called Nova. The Bible tells us that the "Star of Bethlehem" foretold the coming of the birth of Christ and led shepherds, kings, and others to the manger and the new-born King. The Biblical story is traced back over two thousand years to the Old Testament in the Book of Numbers and, according to St. Matthew, in the New Testament.

The "Christmas Star," in truth, is a revered symbol and a favored yuletide tradition.

1976 "Christmas Star"

Reed & Barton's 1976 "Christmas Star" is the first of their annual, limited-edition, hallmarked collection. It is a beautiful, simple, eight-pointed, hollow sterling star. Reed & Barton's interpretation of this time-honored legend is the beginning of an heirloom collection. Each year a sterling and a vermeil star are issued and the dies are officially destroyed at the end of the production run. Designer: George Pinheiro. Dimensions: 2¼″ × 2¼″ w. Issue prices: $8.95 in sterling and vermeil at $12.95.

1977 "Christmas Star"

The poinsettia was the inspiration of the design of the second edition "Christmas Star." The people of Mexico call it the "Flower of the Holy Night" and their legend is that a poor little boy on Christmas Eve long ago went to church and knelt tearfully in prayer, praying of his great desire to give a gift to the Holy Child. When he

The 1979 Ninth Annual Reed and Barton Cross
PHOTO BY REED AND BARTON

The 1976 First Annual Reed and Barton Christmas Star
PHOTO BY REED AND BARTON

The 1977 Second Annual Reed and Barton Christmas Star
PHOTO BY REED AND BARTON

finally stood, at his feet appeared a beautiful green plant with dazzling red flowers—his prayer answered. He joyfully laid blossoms at the feet of Christ at the altar. The plant spread over the country, blooming profusely at Christmastime. The second annual limited "Christmas Star" has a multifaceted holly flower in its center. Designer: John Gilroy. Dimensions: 2¼″ × 2¼″. Issue prices: sterling, $10.00; vermeil, $12.50.

51

1978 "Christmas Star"

The 1978 "Christmas Star" features a jewel-like, multifaceted central decoration surrounded by a silvery, sixteen-pointed sunburst. The alternating levels of raised designs of this year's "Star" serve to capture and reflect every passing light, adding a brilliance and luster to make it both an elegant piece of jewelry and a splendid yuletide decoration.

Reed & Barton's 1978 "Christmas Star" is the third in an annual series of year-marked, limited-edition stars, each to be a unique design, giving added interpretation and richness to this time-honored legend. This sterling-silver original may be worn as a pendant or used as a charming decorative piece to enhance your Christmas wreath, yule tree, or window. Designer: John Gilroy. Dimensions: 2¼″ l × 2½″ w.

1979 "Christmas Star"

Alternating levels of brilliant, sterling silver prisms capture and reflect every passing light in Reed & Barton's 1979 three-dimensional "Christmas Star." It is the fourth of an annual, limited edition of stars. Issue prices: sterling, $10.75; 24 kt. gold electroplate, $13.00. Dimensions: 2½″ h × 1¾″ w.

Holly Ball Collection
Annual Limited Editions

There are several legends surrounding the popular tradition of the use of holly at Christmastime. Holly is symbolic of the Virgin Mary. As Jesus walked the earth it is said that holly sprang up in his footsteps. Holly is supposed to have concealed Christ's presence from his enemies as they sought him. Some believe that the crown of thorns worn by Christ on the cross was made of holly and when pressed on his head, his blood turned the white berries to red. An American custom is a social event of the Christmas season called the "Holly Ball," a dance that is held around the country by many social groups.

Holly is native to most countries and Christian cultures and is treated as a symbol of eternal life, joy, and peace. A Christmas carol has been

The 1978 Third Annual Reed and Barton Christmas Star
PHOTO BY REED AND BARTON

The 1979 Fourth Annual Reed and Barton Christmas Star
PHOTO BY REED AND BARTON

written about it and needless to say, following a century-old tradition, the rich green leaves and brilliant red berries of holly boughs and "Holly Balls" are a favorite yule time decoration around the world. To date, all "Holly Balls" are uniform in size: 3¼" h × 2½" w.

1976 "Holly Ball"

The "Holly Ball," a new tradition, created in silver plate by designer, Gretta Roberts, made its first annual appearance in 1976. This magnificent annual, limited-edition "Holly Ball" has created a new legend and reverence for holly. The 1976 ornament is designed with molded holly leaves and berries at the top and bottom in a swirl effect, is dated on one side, and has "Holly Ball" engraved on the other. (Originally, the "Holly Ball" series was also offered without the year-mark, thus creating two collectables for this issue—dated and undated.) As a collector of these, I would suggest you also get the "undated."

Each year the Reed & Barton craftsmen will create a year-marked limited-edition "Holly Ball" in beautiful silver plate. Issue price: $13.95.

1977 "Holly Ball"

The 1977 "Holly Ball" is more beautiful than the first. It is decorated with a scalloped design of holly leaves and berries and what appears to be petals at the top and bottom of the round "Holly Ball." The loop or ring for hanging the ornament is also different on this issue. Designer: John Gilroy. Issue price: $15.00.

1978 "Holly Ball"

The third "Holly Ball" made a grand entrance into the 1978 Christmas season, profusely designed at the top and bottom with bells, holly, and berries. "Holly Ball" and "1978" are engraved on this ornament and Reed & Barton's hallmark is on the bottom. This designer has created a cherished item to delight generations to come. Issue price: $15.00.

1979 "Holly Ball"

Imagine a pie with a scalloped border, sliced in five wedges, with each wedge separated by three embossed lines tapering down from the center and fanning out to the scalloped edge. Then imagine the five wedges each garnished with one large holly leaf and four berries in various sizes. You have the design of Reed & Barton's 1979 "Holly Ball," number four in this annual collection. Dimension: 2¾" sphere. Issue price: $15.00.

The 1976 First Annual Reed and Barton Holly Ball
PHOTO BY REED AND BARTON

The 1977 Second Annual Reed and Barton Holly Ball
PHOTO BY REED AND BARTON

The 1978 Third Annual Reed and Barton Holly Ball
PHOTO BY REED AND BARTON

The 1979 Fourth Annual Reed and Barton Holly Ball
PHOTO BY REED AND BARTON

Snowflakes Collection

1977 "Snowflakes"

Competition for the "Snowflake" manufacturers came from Reed & Barton with their issue of a first, open lacy-designed pair of "Snowflakes." Each is dated and hallmarked, but each different in design. Both are lovely on my tree and prized in my collection.

I look forward each year to the beauty and originality in all the Reed & Barton collections. Designer: Clark Lofgren. Dimensions: 2¾" h × 2½" w. Issue price: $15.00.

1978 "Snowflakes"

Clark Lofgren sculptured a pair of beautiful, silver-plated and/or vermeil "Snowflakes" to issue for the 1978 holiday season. These lacy "Snowflakes" are individual in design and "related" to each other and the 1977 issues. Dimensions: 2¾" h × 2½" w. Issue prices: silver-plated, $10.00 pair; vermeil, $15.00.

1979 "Snowflakes"

The third annual pair is different in design, but related in feeling. Each see-through design is yearmarked on the back and richly silver-plated. Gift-boxed in pairs. Designer: Clark Lofgren. Dimensions: 2⅜" × 2⅜". Issue Price: $12.50.

Trim-a-Tree Picture Frame Collection

1977 First Annual Limited Edition "Trim-a-Tree Picture Frame" (boxed in pairs and single—silver-plated and vermeil)

A new way to create your "Family Tree" is with a new and unique ornament collection. The ornament, a "Trim-a-Tree Picture Frame," is wreath-styled with holly berries and leaves, and hallmarked with the year of issue. Favorite small photographs can be snapped into the frame behind clear acetate covers, creating a treasured keepsake of family members and friends. My personal goal is to collect enough to have a very

The 1977 First Annual Edition of Two Reed and Barton Snowflakes
PHOTO BY REED AND BARTON

The 1978 Second Annual Edition of Two Reed and Barton Snowflakes
PHOTO BY REED AND BARTON

The 1979 Third Annual Edition of Two Reed and Barton Snowflakes
PHOTO BY REED AND BARTON

special personal tree filled with twenty-four nieces and nephews, assorted cousins, aunts, uncles, five sisters, five brothers-in-law, three brothers, three sisters-in-law, my son Michael, grand-daughter Michele, my husband Joe, my parents and in-laws, etc. Designer: Clark Lofgren. Dimensions: 2½″ h x 2¼″ w. Issue price: single, $6.00; pair, $12.00.

1978 Second Annual "Trim-a-Tree Picture Frame"

A slightly different arrangement of the holly leaves and berries are on the 1978 limited-edition "Picture Frame." It is dated, silver-plated and vermeil. More members will join my "Family Tree" this year.

Reed & Barton also made a "Three Frame Tree" for the desk. Issue prices: single, $6.00; pair, $12.00.

1977–1978 "Trim-a-Tree Stand"

As an added dimension to holiday decor and remembrance, Reed & Barton created an annual "Picture Frame Tree" for 1977 and 1978. The tree created in silver plate or vermeil, is an ornate stand holding three annual, year-marked, "Trim-a-Tree" picture frames to capture for all the time holiday moods of your family and friends. Issue prices: (stand only) silver plate, $15.00; vermeil, $25.00.

1979 Third Annual "Trim-a-Tree Picture Frame"

A circle of vines, leaves and six perching birds is the design of Reed & Barton's 1979 offering in the collection. This year's frame is marked "Noel" on one bottom side and "1979" on the other. Dimensions: 2½″ × 2½″. Issue prices: single, $6.00; pair, $12.00.

The 1977 First Annual Reed and Barton Trim-A-Tree Picture Frames
PHOTO BY REED AND BARTON

The 1978 Second Annual Reed and Barton Trim-A-Tree Picture Frames
PHOTO BY REED AND BARTON

The 1977 First Trim-A-Tree Picture Frame
DISPLAY BY REED AND BARTON

The 1979 Third Annual Reed and Barton Trim-A-Tree Picture Frames
PHOTO BY REED AND BARTON

Tree Castle Collection

The 1977 First Annual Tree Castles by Reed and Barton
PHOTO BY REED AND BARTON

1977 "Christmas Tree Castle"
first edition—20 kt gold finish
Large Cube—Small Cube—Peace Prism

Three delicately sculptured gold-plated Christmas "Tree Castles," airy, three-dimensional, lavishly filigreed were issued as the first editions for this collection in 1977. The "Peace Prism" and "Golden Cubes" provide a new and unique collection to my otherwise basically "Silver Tree." They are profusely detailed with assorted Christmas scenes on the sides of each ornament. Reed & Barton promise to issue a completely new series of copyrighted "Tree Castles" year after year, and some day I will have a "Tree Castle" Christmas Tree!

Designers: cooperative effort. Dimensions: large cube—2¼″ h × 2¼″ w, small cube—1½″ h × 1⅛″ w, peace prism—4½″ h × 2″ w. Issue prices: large cube—$12.50, small cube—$9.00, peace prism—$12.50.

1978 "Christmas Tree Castle"
(Second Edition—20 kt Gold Finish)

Two stylized "Gazebo" ornaments are the 1978 offerings in Reed & Barton's "Tree Castle" collection. The gold-plated, filigreed additions are beautifully sculptured in scenes of "Choir" and "Nativity," as they are called, and are two more examples of Reed & Barton's promise of a "golden" unique collection. Designed cooperatively by Reed & Barton designers. Dimensions: "Choir" is 2⅝″ h; "Nativity" is 2¾″ h. Issue price: $10.00 each.

The 1978 Second Annual Tree Castles by Reed and Barton
PHOTO BY REED AND BARTON

1979 "Christmas Tree Castle"
(third edition — 24 kt. gold wash)

Elegant, airy and intricately filigreed in 24 kt gold wash are the two offerings for 1979 in this collection. Dimensions: "Peace Dove" is 3¾″ h; "Holly" is 4¼″ h. Issue price: $10.00 each.

"Twelve Days of Christmas Bells"

1977 "Partridge" & "Turtle Dove"

The "Twelve Days of Christmas" is one of the most festive of Christmas carols and has been inspirational to several silversmith companies in creating Christmas ornament series. I must say here that I have four collections of "Twelve Days" ornaments, each made by a different company and each collection very unique. I can forsee that some day an entire large tree can be decorated with "Twelve Days" series.

The new series created by Reed & Barton is done in miniature bells. The annual, unlimited collection began in 1977 in pairs, representing the first and second days of Christmas, "A Pert-Tailed European Partridge and a graceful Turtle Dove, each Perched Atop its Own Bell." Each Christmas season in the coming years, Reed & Barton will issue a new pair of "Twelve Days Bells" until the "carol" is complete. The bells are silver-plated, unlimited, and undated. According to Reed & Barton "there is no 'correct' version of the sequence of the 'gifts' in this centuries-old folk carol, particularly for days eight through 12." Reed & Barton will coordinate this "Twelve Days" with Towle's:

Reed and Barton's 12 Days of Christmas Bells   1978
Three French Hens and Four Calling Birds
PHOTO BY REED & BARTON

1978 Three French Hens and Four Colly
      Birds
1979 Five Golden Rings and Six Geese
      A-Laying
1980 Seven Swans A-Swimming and Eight
      Lords A-Leaping
1981 Nine Ladies Dancing and Ten Pipers
      Piping
1982 Eleven Drummers Drumming and
      Twelve Maids A-Milking

This is a nice collection for the "impatient" collector—ending the same year Towle's "Twelve Days" are scheduled to end. Designer: Clark Lofgren. Dimensions: Partridge, 2½″ h; Dove, 2¾″ h. Issue prices: 1977, $12.50 a pair; 1978, $15.00 a pair.

Twelve Days of Christmas Bells

The first six of this "Twelve Days of Christmas" collection were issued in 1979 as a set in a red-velvet-lined gift box, allowing the collector who missed them in 1978 and 1979 to catch up. Issue price: $52.00. A wooden shelf designed to house the entire dozen was also made available.

1978 "Three French Hens" & "Four Colly Birds"

An antique-finished French Hen is nesting on shiny, silver plated bell number three and one Colly Bird, representing bell four, is proudly perched on another for 1978's representation of Reed & Barton's "Twelve Days of Christmas Bells." Issue price: $17.50 a pair.

1979 "Five Golden Rings & Six Geese-A-Laying"

Five gold plated, interwoven rings are the handle for the fifth bell and is the first form of something other than a bird, as well as a change in metals, with the mixing of gold and silver. In bell number 6, the birds are back with a laying goose and an egg as evidence. Issue price: $17-.50 a pair.

Twelve Days Bells Second Pair 1978 by Reed and Barton
PHOTO BY REED AND BARTON

Twelve Days Bell First Three Pairs by Reed and Barton
PHOTO BY REED AND BARTON

1977   *1979*   *1978*

Reed and Barton Traditional Bell

Reed and Barton 1979 Traditional Bell

Reed and Barton Music Makers

Collection of Bells by Reed and Barton

1979 (first edition) *"Prisms"*
"Snowflake & Starlight"

A pair of "Prisms" was made available in 1979 by Reed & Barton. The geometric and futuristic design was created to give dancing reflections from lights. "Snowflake" is an open, airy mesh look, with a snowflake in each prism. "Starlight" is made of solid panels. Diameter: 2½″. Issue price: rodium-plated or 24 kt. gold wash, $10.00.

Reed and Barton Prisms

___ 6 ___
The Lunt Silversmiths Collections

Trefoils, Flowers of Christmas,
Songs of Christmas, and the Tiny Tots

The Lunt Silversmiths, Roger, Lunt & Bowen Company, is one of "direct heritage of fine silversmithing for over two hundred fifty years!" Members of the Lunt family are still continuing this heritage. Mr. George C. Lunt assisted me by furnishing the picture shown in the "Lunt" chapter.

Trefoils (Limited Edition)

"Shepherds Vigil" 1972

The first limited-edition ornament offered by Lunt is called the "Shepherds Vigil" and was designed by Lunt's craftsmen and issued during the 1972 Christmas season. The intricately designed Trefoil-shaped, sterling medallion is hallmarked, dated, and open-cut. It shows two shepherds following a star, with a cross in its design, to the city of Bethlehem seen in the distance. It is the beginning of a collection of four in this series. They will never be repeated. Dimensions of all in collection: 2¾ × 2¾. Issue price: $10.00.

"Gift of Kings" 1973

Three Kings, again trefoil-shaped, called the "Gift of Kings," produced in 1973 is the second of this series. The three wise men following the

Lunt Silversmiths First Edition Trefoil
"Shepherds Vigil" 1972 PHOTO BY LUNT

star of Bethlehem are so masterfully engraved on this ornament that you feel the richness of their garments, crowns, and scepters. How I wish Lunt had continued this series! Issue price: $12.50.

"Journey by Starlight" 1974

The 1974 Christmas medallion, third in this series, called "Journey by Starlight" is a work of art. It captures the true meaning of Christmas. Mary rides the donkey, led by Joseph on foot, into the city of Bethlehem under the protective light of a brilliant star. The city in the distance will have "no room in the inn" for the soon to be born King of Kings, Lord of Lords! Issue price: $13.95.

"First Christmas" 1975

The final trefoil ornament in this collection produced in 1975 is called the "First Christmas." You can almost hear the angels singing, know the joy and feel the peace depicted on this medallion. Christ the Savior is Born; it is our first Christmas. Mary holds the infant Jesus, as Joseph stands by. The cattle of the lowly manger are in the background. A collection to treasure. Issue price: $15.00. Collection closed.

Lunt Silversmiths 1973 "Gift Of Kings"
PHOTO BY LUNT

Lunt Silversmiths 1974 "Journey By Starlight"
PHOTO BY LUNT

Lunt Silversmiths 1975 "First Christmas"
Collection Closed PHOTO BY LUNT

Flowers of Christmas Collection
(Limited Edition)

"Mistletoe" 1976

"Mistletoe" is the name of the first of this series. Issued in 1976, this hollow, round ornament has a lovely mistletoe branch encircled by holly leaves on one side. A beautifully sculptured snowflake is on the other side. To wear this as jewelry is an invitation to be kissed!!! Dimensions for both years: 2¼ × 2¼. Issue price: $15.00.

"Holly Wreath" 1977

The fine craftsmen of Lunt Silversmiths fashioned a "Holly Wreath" to adorn the tree in 1977. This second edition of the "Flowers of Christmas" clearly shows every detail of the holly leaves, berries, pine cones, and a big bow on one side, and on the other the snowflake of 1976 makes its second appearance. Issue price: $15.00.

(A new hallmark dated "Flower" will be issued in 1978, and I have a hunch the snowflake will be back again. Collection closed.)

Lunt Silversmiths 1976 Flowers Of Christmas Collection First Edition "Mistletoe"
PHOTO BY LUNT

Lunt Silversmiths 1977 Flowers Of Christmas Collection "Holly Wreath" Second Edition
PHOTO BY LUNT

Music of Christmas Collection
(Limited Edition)

"Jingle Bells" 1976

"Jingle Bells" is the first offering by Lunt, in
1976, of their "Music of Christmas" collection.
The notes of this popular song are actually
scored on a partially rolled music sheet, adorned
with a boy, bells, and holly leaves on one side of
this medallion. The other side is hallmarked and
dated. Issue price: $15.00.

"Silent Night" 1977

Franz Gruber wrote "Silent Night" in 1818 in a
little Austrian village called Oberndorf. I know
this because in 1977 the craftsmen at Lunt
created a second-edition, sterling-silver ornament, named it "Silent Night," and engraved this
information on one side of it. On the other side,
they engraved the notes of this beautiful carol
and sculptured a scene showing the small parish
church where on Christmas Eve, 1818, the world
first heard this lovely melody. Dimensions for all
"Music" ornaments are the same: 2½" h × 2" w.
    Both issues of this collection are oval shaped
and cut-out, and I am excited about the future
issues! Issue price: $15.00.

Lunt Silversmiths 1976 First Edition
"Music of Christmas" "Jingle Bells"
PHOTO BY LUNT

Lunt Silversmiths 1977 Music of Christmas
Second Edition "Silent Night" PHOTO BY LUNT

"O Christmas Tree" 1978

"O Tree of Green Un-Changing—You Set My Heart A-Singing," a verse from the loved Christmas carol "O Christmas Tree," is engraved on one side of Lunt's third edition, the 1978 offering of their sterling-silver "Music of Christmas" collection. Also on the back of this ornament is a decorated Christmas tree bearing the year "1978" and a scroll-like banner engraved with "O Tannenbaum." Children, five of them, are rejoicing around the tree on the front of this ornament, with the music of this "Carol" scored around the border. The shape and size of this ornament are the same as both earlier editions. Issue price: $15.00.

"Joy To The World" 1979

The word "Joy," spelled out with each letter profusely decorated with scrolling designs that continue around the border, is the focal point of the fourth edition in this collection of Christmas carols. An open book seems to be a supporting base for "Joy." It has "Joy To The World" written on the left page, and the actual musical score of this favorite carol is written on the right page. A candle and date "1979" are final touches. This lilting carol was written by Isaac Watts in 1719 and set to music by G. F. Handel in 1745. Issue price: $32.75.

Lunt Silversmith 1978 Music of Christmas Third Edition "O' Tannenbaum" Reverse Side
PHOTO BY LUNT

Front Side of Lunt Silversmiths 1978 Third Edition of Music of Christmas "O' Tennenbaum"
PHOTO BY LUNT

The 1978 "Christmas Wreath" by Lunt Silver Co.
PHOTO BY LUNT

Lunt Silversmiths 1979 Music of Christmas
Third Edition "Joy to the World"
PHOTO BY LUNT

Tiny Tots

"Little Folks" 1976
"Sleepy Heads" 1977

These special little ornaments are not limited but are annual and small enough to be used as charms. "Little Folks," a pair of small ornaments, were introduced in 1976. "A Little Girl" is holding on to a small Christmas tree and a "Little Boy" is clutching a wrapped gift. The 1977 "Sleepy Heads" shows the "Little Girl" hugging her teddy bear while the "Little Boy" is holding a night candle. Both appear to have had a busy day and they really are "Sleepy Heads." Issue price: $6.00 each. Collection closed.

Lunt Silversmiths 1976 "Little Folks"
PHOTO BY LUNT

Lunt Silversmiths 1977 "Sleepy Heads" (Closed)
PHOTO BY LUNT

65

In 1978 Lunt changed its style of ornaments relating to Christmas greenery by issuing a first-edition ornament called a "Wreath." The "Wreath" is a sterling-silver, flat, coin-shaped ornament with open scroll-work bordering it. The front has an ivory, disc inset that is designed in its center in a stained-glass-type wreath, green of holly, leaves, red berries, pine cones, and a big, beautiful, red ribbon tied in a bow. The solid sterling back is engraved with "1978," "Merry Christmas," and "Sterling Frame by Lunt." Issue price: $15.00.

(All Lunt designs are a cooperative effort of their design department, Emil Schoedel, director.)

"Evergreen" 1979

"Evergreen" is a colorful Christmas medallion mounted on a sterling silver frame by Lunt. Each bough, each ornament, so perfect in detail! The tiny ornaments seem to glow and glisten by themselves. This original design was developed by Lunt Craftsmen. Issue price: $26.50.

Lunt Silversmiths 1978 First Edition "Christmas Wreath"
PHOTO BY LUNT

Lunt Silversmith 1978 Reverse Side of 1978
"Christmas Wreath" PHOTO BY LUNT

Lunt Silversmiths 1979 Christmas Wreath
Second Edition "Evergreen"
PHOTO BY LUNT

— 7 —
The Samuel Kirk & Sons Collections

Cherub
The Christmas Angel
The Christmas Music Bell Collection (Music Bell Playing)

The oldest surviving silversmith company in the United States is Samuel Kirk & Sons, Inc., founded by Samuel Kirk in 1815 in Baltimore, Maryland.

Kirk, a prestigious company, is known the world over as a leader in magnificent craftsmanship and their Repoussé design. There are Kirk family members at the helm of the company today. Kirk has designed many famous presentation pieces and trophies, including a 248-piece dinner service for the Maryland cruiser in 1905, now housed at the State House at Annapolis.

In 1972 Kirk, under the direction of Robert F. Welzenbach, plant manager, designers, Mat Peloso and Donald Bacorn and others joined the ranks of producing limited, annual, silver Christmas ornaments, creating another form of "Family Heritage" for Americans.

Cherub 1973

"Cherub" on a chain, designed by Mat Peloso (no longer with Kirk) was offered at Christmastime 1973. The sterling "Cherub," doubling as an ornament or pendant, is a delightful little winged, naked offering, holding a finely etched bow-topped wreath. Dies retired 1973. Issue price: $20.00.

Samuel Kirk and Sons' Star   PHOTO BY KEVIN NASH

Christmas Angel 1972

A large, disc-shaped flat, sterling Christmas ornament was issued in 1972 by Kirk. The front, in a combination of dull and polished finish, has an engraved, cupid-like, winged angel blowing a horn (it appears to be masculine and to be walking). The date "1972," "S. Kirk & Son" and "Sterling" are engraved on the back. Simple but elegant. Designer: Donald Bacorn. Dies retired. Dimensions: Kirk star, 2¼" h × 2⅜" w; Kirk angel, 2½" h × 2½" w. Issue price: $20.00

Musical Bells — Christmas Carols

"Jingle Bells" 1977

The Kirk Company, being a leader in silversmithing, wanted to produce something significantly "Christmas" but different from the tree ornaments offered at the time. Then the idea of a bell that would actually play music came and so did tremendous success! This first-edition "Christmas Music Bell" of 1977 I believe will be one of the most sought after, elusive ornaments of all time. It was a sleeper and most dealers and collectors did not hear of it until the 1977 Christmas day had passed.

I did not realize it was "limited and annual" until January 1978! I then pursued it nationwide without results but am happy to say I now have two in my collection. Another interesting point is that Kirk made approximately 20,000 copies of this bell of which 10,000 play "Jingle Bells" and 10,000 play the *first lines* only of "Jingle Bells," making two collectible versions of this issue!

I have both. The bell, made of fine-crafted silver plate, contains a hand-assembled music box that plays "Jingle Bells", is hallmarked and dated and will never be repeated. Find it, if you can. Designer: Donald Bacorn. Dimension: 3". Issue price: $15.00.

"White Christmas" 1978

The 1978 edition of the annual "Music Bell" by Kirk plays "White Christmas" and the second

Samuel Kirk and Sons' Cherub
PHOTO BY KEVIN NASH

The Samuel Kirk and Sons' First Annual (1977) Music Bell
PHOTO BY KIRK

bell is designed with a snowflake, is dated and hallmarked.

Each year the designer/craftsmen at Kirk will issue a "Christmas Music Bell" with a music box inside that will brighten the holiday season with music. These annual, silver-plated bells will be hallmarked, dated, designed with a Christmas motif, and never repeated. A melodious collection of Christmas carols. Designer: Donald Bacorn. Dimensions: 3". Issue price: $17.95.

Samuel Kirk and Sons' 1978 Second Edition
"Christmas Music Bell"   "Snowflake"
PHOTO BY KIRK

"Deck the Halls" 1979

The 1979 Kirk Musical Bell is the third of a series of an annual issue by Samuel Kirk & Sons. Crafted in fine silver plate, the musical bell contains a hand-assembled music box that plays the Holiday tune "Deck the Halls." There are three ringing bells, amid holly leaves, and the year of issue, 1979, is engraved on the bell. Dimension: 3″. Issue price: $17.50.

The Samuel Kirk & Sons Company and the Steiff Company have merged as of 1979. They are now known as "The Kirk Steiff Company/Silversmiths — Goldsmiths — Pewterers.

70

8

The Hamilton Mint Collection

Snowflakes

A set of four sterling-silver snowflakes were introduced in 1976. Each one measures approximately 3½″ in size. These snowflakes were specially lacquered for maximum luster and to make them tarnish proof. Issue price was $30.00.

These ornaments could not be ordered separately, as the Lincoln Mint set of 1972 could, but then again, the Lincoln ornaments were much more expensive.

The mint offered four completely different designs for 1977. As before, the set of four had to be purchased complete. The 1977 edition price was $35.00.

None of the ornaments are marked either with the manufacturer's name or any date. The box the ornament sets came in is not marked either.

"First Snowflake Collection" 1976

Snowflake, Thin Star Center, Six Pinhole Ends—Issue price: $7.50
Snowflake, Thin Star Center, Twelve Rectangular End Holes—Issue price: $7.50
Snowflake, Triple Hexagonal Center Design—Issue price: $7.50
Snowflake, Thin Star Center, Arrows Pointing Inward—Issue price: $7.50

"Second Snowflake Collection" 1977

Snowflake, Single Hexagonal Center Design, Arrow Feather Ends—Issue price: $8.75
Snowflake, Star Center, 12 Large Barbed Points—Issue price: $8.75.
Snowflake, Thin Star Center, 18 Small Barbed Ends—Issue price: $8.75.
Snowflake, Wide Star Center, 18 Large Barbed Ends—Issue price: $8.75.

Hamilton Mint's 1976 First Collection of Four Snowflakes

Hamilton Mint's 1977 Second Collection of Four Snowflakes

The 1971–Silent Night, First of the Hamilton Mint's Christmas Carol Collection.
PHOTO BY THE HAMILTON MINT

O' Come All Ye Faithful, 1973 Third Edition by The Hamilton Mint.
PHOTO BY HAMILTON MINT

First Noel 1972 Second Edition by The Hamilton Mint.
PHOTO BY HAMILTON MINT

The 1974 Hark The Herald Angels Sing, Fourth Edition Christmas Carol by The Hamilton Mint.
PHOTO BY THE HAMILTON MINT

The 1975 O' Little Town of Bethlehem, Fifth Edition by The Hamilton Mint.
PHOTO BY THE HAMILTON MINT

The 1976 It Came Upon A Midnight Clear, Sixth Edition by The Hamilton Mint
PHOTO BY THE HAMILTON MINT

The 1977 O' Holy Night, Seventh Edition by The Hamilton Mint.
PHOTO BY THE HAMILTON MINT

74

_9_
The Franklin Mint Corporation Collection

Franklin Center, located in Pennsylvania's historic Brandywine River Valley near Philadelphia, is headquarters for the world's largest private mint and leading producer of limited-edition collectibles. The corporation's international subsidiaries include John Pinches, Ltd., British medalists whose history dates back to 1840; the Franklin Mint Canada, Ltd., Canada's largest private mint; and Le Medaillier, S.A., a French company. The company is owned by more than ten thousand shareholders.

The Franklin Mint, located at corporate headquarters in Franklin Center, is the company's principal operating division. Here, sterling silver is melted and cast in a continuous operation, capable of processing more than one hundred million ounces of silver a year.

Adjacent to the mint is The Franklin Mint Museum, which contains one of the world's largest collections of proof-quality coins, medals, ingots, and additional collectors' items produced in gold, silver, and other materials. The museum, built especially to house the world's most complete collection of Franklin Mint issues, was opened in 1973. Since then more than 100,000 visitors a year have toured The Franklin Mint Museum.

"Twelve Days of Christmas"

The first known, limited-edition, sterling-silver Christmas ornaments produced in the United States were made available through subscriptions by the Franklin Mint Corporation, Franklin Mint Division of Franklin Center, Pennsylvania, in 1966 and 1970.

The collection of twelve ornaments depicting the famous carol, "Twelve Days of Christmas" is called the "Christmas Heirloom Edition" and was sculptured by artist, Carlos Sierra-Franco. Each ornament is a silver-dollar-size sterling coin, beautifully sculptured in the artist's interpretation of the appropriate day of Christmas on one side and the number of the day centered in a sunburst design on the other.

Each coin, encased in tear-drop-shaped, clear lucite, is 6″ long and 2½″ wide. When hanging from the Christmas tree branches, this collection gives the impression of magnificent coins suspended in midair! The set came packaged in a simulated, blue leather case and one thousand sets were minted at $150.00 for the set or $12.50 per ornament. This collection was also offered to Franklin Mint subscribers in a solid platinum edition, would you believe for a mere $15,000.00? There were no takers.

Franklin Mint's First Day of the Twelve Days of Christmas   PHOTO BY KEVIN NASH

The Franklin Mint's Fourth Day of Christmas

The Franklin Mint's Second Day of Christmas

The Franklin Mint's Fifth Day of Christmas

The Franklin Mint's Third Day of Christmas

The Franklin Mint's Sixth Day of Christmas

The Franklin Mint's Seventh Day of Christmas

The Franklin Mint's Tenth Day of Christmas

The Franklin Mint's Eighth Day of Christmas

The Franklin Mint's Eleventh Day of Christmas

The Franklin Mint's Ninth Day of Christmas

The Franklin Mint's Twelfth Day of Christmas

Center Coins of the Franklin Mint's First Day of Christmas

The Reverse Side of the First Day of Christmas by the Franklin Mint PHOTO BY KEVIN NASH

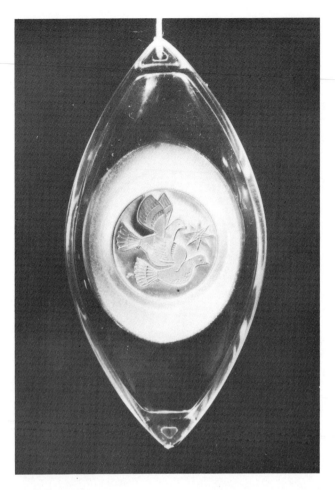

Center Coins of the Second Day of Christmas

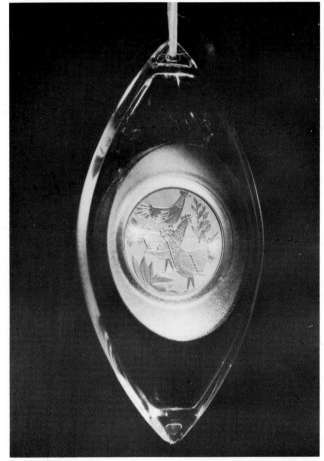

Center Coins of the Third Day of Christmas

Center Coins of the Fourth Day of Christmas

Center Coins of the Fifth Day of Christmas

81

Center Coins of the Sixth Day of Christmas

Center Coins of the Seventh Day of Christmas

82

Center Coins of the Eighth Day of Christmas

Center Coins of the Ninth Day of Christmas

Center Coins of the Tenth Day of Christmas

Center Coins of the Eleventh Day of Christmas

Center Coins of the Twelfth Day of Christmas

The Franklin Mint began its second annual series of limited-edition ornaments called the "Christmas Carol Collection" in 1971. The collection, designed to capture the spirit of famous Christmas carols is executed in sterling-silver, seven-pointed stars centered with a magnificently sculptured sterling coin depicting a theme of the "Carol" and inscribed with the name of the carol, the issue year date, and is in a colored round lucite halo. Because these ornaments are and were sold by subscription only, the minted numbers vary from year to year, determined by subscriptions, creating highly sought after ornaments of the low mintage years.

"Silent Night" 1971

"Mother and Child" is depicted on the "Silent Night" first edition in 1971. Mother Mary tenderly holds sleeping baby Jesus in a seven-pointed sterling star encased in a blue lucite holder. Sculptor: Richard Baldwin. Mintage: 14,683. Issue price: $30.00.

"First Noel" 1972

In 1972, sculptor Norman Nemeth and designer Joseph Aita created a beautiful angel with clasped hands and magnificent widespread wings as the center focus of the "First Noel" carol ornament in red lucite. Mintage: 14,436. Issue price: $30.00.

"O Come All Ye Faithful" 1973

The three wise men bearing gifts, followed by shepherds and others, seeking to honor the newborn king are shown on the third offering of the Franklin Mint which is encased in red lucite. Sculptor: James Ferrell; designer, Ernest Schroeder. Mintage: 14,816. Issue price: $30.00.

"Hark! The Herald Angels Sing" 1974

Jane Lunger designed and sculptured six angels, heralding the birth of Christ while hovering over the tiny city of Bethlehem, thus making the "Hark! The Herald Angels Sing," fourth edition of the Christmas Carol Collection, encased in green lucite. Mintage: 12,229. Issue price: $40.00.

"O Little Town of Bethlehem" 1975

Lavender lucite surrounds the sterling "O Little Town of Bethlehem," fifth-edition ornament of 1975. The design, a collaboration of sculptor Jane Lunger and designer David Bonner shows Mary riding the donkey led by Joseph and entering Bethlehem. The low mintage of this year's edition of only 7,626 has caused the present-day cost to increase from the issue price of $47.50 to not less than $175.00, if you are fortunate enough to find it!

"It Came Upon a Midnight Clear" 1976

A finely etched, majestic angel adorns the beautiful 1976 ornament titled "It Came Upon a Midnight Clear." This, the sixth edition of the Christmas Carol Collection is encased in blue lucite. Sculptor: Yves Beaujard; designer, Jane Lunger. Mintage: 6,633. Issue price: $47.50.

"O Holy Night" 1977

Donald Everhart, designer and sculptor, created a scene of shepherds tending their flock, with the holy city seen on the hill in the distance. His interpretation of the 1977 seventh-edition ornament is called "O Holy Night." The lucite halo is deep pink. Mintage: Not available. Issue price: $55.00.

Snowflake Treetopping and Christmas Cherub Ornaments 1977

In 1977, the Franklin Mint also produced two silver ornaments: The Christmas Cherub (angel blowing horn). Issue price: $65.00. Treetop Snowflake, Dimension: 5½". Issue price: $75.00.

"The Blessing" 1978

"The Blessing" features a solid, sterling silver, art medal designed especially for Christmas of 1978. The medal, centered in a sterling pointed star, is surrounded by a beautiful golden, lucite halo measuring 4″ in diameter. The medal features Mother Mary kneeling at the Baby Jesus' manger. Issue price: $55.00.

10
The Danbury Mint Collection

The Danbury Mint, formed in August 1969, is a division of MBI, Inc., which is a privately owned corporation with headquarters in Norwalk, Connecticut. MBI, Inc. is a subsidiary of Glendinning Companies, Inc. of Westport. The business of MBI, Inc. is direct marketing of quality collectors' items. In their formative years, the Danbury Mint marketed mainly coins, medals, medallions, and ingots. As of 1976, other collectors' items, such as porcelain and crystal bells, porcelain plate, crystal and pewter sculptures, and more importantly to this author, gold, limited and annual editions of Christmas ornaments. Many collectors in 1976 wrote the Danbury Mint to express their delight with their first Christmas ornament. A number of them came forward with the suggestion that instead of issuing one new ornament per year, the Danbury Mint issue one ornament per *month* beginning early enough so collectors might acquire a number of additional different, yet similar ornaments in time for Christmas 1977. The Mint's response was:

1) The Danbury Mint would issue a collection of *twelve* gold-covered ornaments, in a strictly limited edition.

2) They would be available only by subscription for reservations postmarked by February 28, 1977.
3) Each ornament would be individually hallmarked and registered.
4) Their status as an exclusive collector's item would be assured in that only established collectors of the Danbury Mint were offered this opportunity to subscribe. This edition would *not* be available to *anyone* else.
5) The original issue price was $12.50 per ornament, the same price as the first Christmas ornament, and this price was guaranteed for all twelve ornaments in this collection.

Each ornament was handcrafted for the Danbury Mint by Reed and Barton Silversmiths, of Taunton, Massachusetts. Each was struck in metal, electroplated with a heavy coating of 20 k gold, then hand-polished to a brilliant luster, and placed in a beautiful display box.

This collection of three-dimensional ornaments came about in a "request" manner, to go with the Mint's "first" ornament issued in 1976—thus another collection was born in 1977 that has eluded this author, since I was not a subscriber at that time.

Angels

"Annual Angel" Christmas Ornament 1976

The very first Christmas ornament, made available by the Danbury Mint to only their subscribers, was created exclusively for them by Reed & Barton Silversmiths, in 20 k electrogoldplate and was a three-dimensional "Angel."

As the years pass, the first Danbury Mint gold Christmas ornament will always evoke cherished memories of Christmas 1976, and it will surely become a treasured heirloom—not only because of its beauty but also because of its rarity.

It was a *limited edition,* available at the original issue price only for orders postmarked before December 25, 1976. Each fine gold-covered ornament was hallmarked and registered. Its status as an exclusive collectors' item will be protected in that absolutely *none* were made available to retail stores. It came with its registration, gift boxed, and issued at $12.50 plus shipping costs. It is 3⅝" h and was the Danbury Mint's entrance into the very popular field of annual and limited Christmas ornaments.

"Annual Angel" Christmas Ornament 1977

The second-edition, annual, limited gold-plated "Angel" Christmas ornament was created at Reed and Barton exclusively for the Danbury Mint. The "Angel" was made available only to the Mint subscribers at $13.50 in 1977 and is 3¾" h.

The "Angel", three-dimensional in design, is four angels, soldered facing each other with their faces lifted toward the heavens and blowing their horns. The edition closed December 25, 1977.

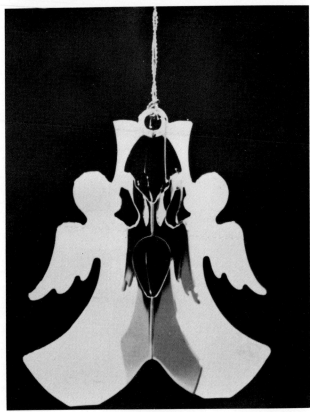

The Danbury Mint's 1976 First Annual Angel

The Danbury Mint's 1977 Second Annual Angel
PHOTO BY KEVIN NASH

The Danbury Mint's 1978 Third Annual Angel

The Danbury Mint's Christmas Tree
From the Collection of Twelve 1977

The Annual Twelve Ornament Set

First Collection of Twelve 1977
Gold Christmas Ornaments

"Christmas Tree" (#1)

The "first" in the Danbury Mint's first collection of twelve 20 k gold electroplated ornaments, issued to subscribers in a limited edition and registered in the owner's name was the "Christmas Tree." All ornaments in this collection are similar in classic design, three-dimensional, come with a gold cord for hanging, and are approximately 3 5/8″ h. All were issued at $12.50 each plus shipping charges.

"Bell" (#2)

The "Bell" is actually a collection of bells and clappers, creatively designed to appear to be "ringing," by Reed and Barton exclusively for the Danbury Mint.

"Star" (#3)

Another "Star" is born. It is number three in this Mint's collection of twelve golden ornaments for 1977. This version of the "Star of Bethlehem" has eighteen points and a cord for hanging on the Christmas tree.

"Candle" (#4)

Years ago, real candles were used to light the Christmas tree. At an appointed time of the day, the entire family gathered around to watch as a member would carefully light the candles and delight at their glowing, illuminated tree. They would then snuff them out until the next day for the same appointed time. Number four in this collection of twelve is the "Candle," recalling those happy memories.

89

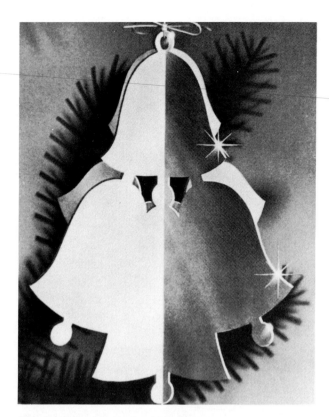

The Danbury Mint's Jingle Bells
From First Collection of Twelve 1977

The Danbury Mint's Christmas Star
First Collection of Twelve 1977

"Partridge" (#5)

As far as I know the 'Partridge" recalls the Christmas carol, however, this one will recall the year 1977 for its owners, when it was issued by the Danbury Mint as number five in their first collection of twelve golden ornaments.

"Snowman" (#6)

Usually a "Snowman" is white, but this three-dimensional one is a golden Christmas tree ornament and is number six in this collection of registered, limited ornaments.

"Church" (#7)

To date I know of only two "Church" ornaments, one in sterling and this one in 20 k electroplated gold. It is the seventh in a collection of twelve issued in 1977 by the Danbury Mint.

"Teddy Bear" (#8)

My son would not take his naps nor be tucked in bed at night without his "Teddy Bear," now number eight in this collection. The "Teddy Bear," which came into being as a result of one of our presidents, Theodore "Teddy" Roosevelt, is now a favorite toy and Christmas tree ornament.

"Jingle Bells" (#9)

"Jingle Bells" is as much a part of Christmas as apple pie is American. They are on Santa's sleigh, on the horses' collars, and are a beautiful sound as they go "dashing thru the snow." Now as number nine in this collection of twelve, they are a golden edition on the tree for lucky subscribers of 1977.

The Danbury Mint's Candle
First Collection of Twelve 1977

The Danbury Mint's The Partridge
First Collection of Twelve 1977

"Wreath" (#10)

Windows and doors bearing a Christmas "Wreath" during the holiday season are a warm welcome sight and emit the joy within to passersby. This one in gold is number ten in the Danbury Mint's first collection of twelve ornaments, issued in 1977.

"Reindeer" (#11)

Since this is the first of its kind from the Danbury Mint, perhaps it's Rudolph the red-nosed "Reindeer." It is number eleven and was issued in gold plate in 1977 as a part of a collection of twelve. I do hope that the Mint and Reed & Barton will see to it that the other seven tiny "Reindeer" that pull Santa's sleigh will join this one in future years.

"Snowflake" (#12)

Number twelve in this collection of twelve, limited edition, electroplated 20 k gold ornaments for the Danbury Mint subscribers issued in 1977 is a three-dimensional "Snowflake." It is the first "Snowflake" offered by the Mint, three others, all different in design, joined this one in 1978.

Second Limited Edition
Collection of Twelve 1978

Only one family in thousands could own the exquisitively crafted, harmoniously designed, and lastingly beautiful Christmas ornaments in this timeless heirloom collection.

Generations ago, our forebears might have purchased such ornaments from a village craftsman who created them as a labor of love. Today, the village craftsman is rarely to be found and so ornaments of this quality are also rare.

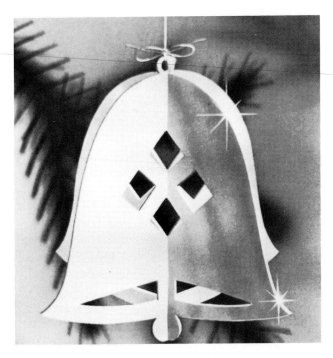

The Danbury Mint's The Church Bell
First Collection of Twelve 1977

The Danbury Mint issued a new collection of twelve beautiful, gold-covered Christmas ornaments, each one brilliantly expressing the joy of the holiday season and designed originally and exclusively for this collection. Each ornament is handcrafted in metal and then electroplated with a heavy coating of 20 k gold by Reed and Barton Silversmiths of Taunton, Massachusetts, and are individually hallmarked and registered.

The collection was issued only once (1978) in a strictly limited private edition—available only to registered Danbury Mint collectors who submitted their reservations no later than February 28, 1978. The subscriber rolls were then closed forever. These ornaments will never again be available. Dimension: 3⅝″ h each ornament. The original issue price was $13.50 per ornament.

"The Lantern" (#1)

The "Lantern" calls to mind the strolling carolers singing the joys of Christmas in the town square in the days of yore with the "lanterns" lighting their way. It is one of the twelve ornaments in 20 k gold, limited edition series issued exclusively by the Danbury Mint, 1978. The "Lantern" is three-dimensional and 3⅝″ h.

The Danbury Mint's Lantern
Second Collection of Twelve 1978

The "Holly", in 20 k gold electroplate symbolizes the traditional decoration that "decks the halls, windows, gifts, and doors" of homes during the holiday season. It is 3¾" h, three-dimensional, and one of the 1978 "Twelve" from the Danbury Mint's limited edition series.

"The Hobbyhorse" (#3)

Remember the "Hobbyhorse" like the one many little sleepy heads dreamed of on Christmas Eve? They hoped to find one under the tree on Christmas morn and now a select few collectors have the "Hobbyhorse" hanging on their trees. It was made available by the Danbury Mint in 20 k electrogold plate in 1978, another of the twelve of their limited edition series at 3¾" h.

"The Bell and Bow" (#4)

Four "Bells," tied at the top with a "Bow," with ribbons falling from the "Bow" to the base, is another of the Danbury Mint's "Twelve" in 1978 limited series. Created in 20 k electrogold plate, it is 4" h.

"The Snowflake" (#5)

The "Snowflake," number five, is an interpretation created by Reed and Barton for the Danbury Mint's collection of twelve gold-plated ornaments in their 1978 limited-edition series. It is a contemporary, gleaming, multipointed beautiful addition, made available to a fortunate few, and will be repeated, as will all others in this collection. 3¾"h.

The Danbury Mint's Holly
Second Collection of Twelve 1978

The Danbury Mint's Hobby Horse
Second Collection of Twelve 1978

The Danbury Mint's Bell with Bow
Second Collection of Twelve 1978

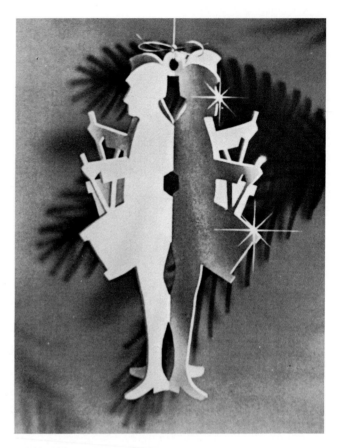

The Danbury Mint's Drummer Boy
Second Collection of Twelve 1978

The Danbury Mint's Snowflake
Second Collection of Twelve 1978

"The Drummer Boy" (#6)

The "Drummer Boy" appears to be four drummer boys with their backs connected, with each of them beating a drum. Standing 3¾" h, in electrogold plate, they are "drumming up" a beautiful holiday season in 1978, and years to come, for the Danbury Mint and all of their lucky owners. Available only in 1978 and only to subscribers.

"Snowflake II" (#7)

Since no two snowflakes are alike and we all "dream of a white Christmas," the Danbury Mint chose to have three snowflakes in the 1978 collection of twelve. This, the gold "Snowflake II," is harmoniously designed for this collection, similar in size and has its own gold cord for hanging.

"Candy Cane" (#8)

The "Candy Cane" is a traditional part of Christmas. "Candy Canes" have for many years been a part of tree decoration, and in 1978 a gold one created by Reed and Barton for the Danbury Mint became a part of their "collection of twelve."

"Ragdoll" (#9)

Recalling the pioneer years of our country when people secretly hand made the gifts they lovingly placed under the tree for family members, the golden "Ragdoll," that delighted many little girls is number 9 in the Danbury Mint's collection of 12 for 1978.

"Poinsettia" (#10)

The "Poinsettia," with its own legend dating back to the birth of Christ, is a holiday favorite around the world at the Christmas season and is number 10 in the Danbury Mint's collection of 12 for 1978.

"Jack-in-the-Box" (#11)

We all love the funny little clown that pops out of a box, so number eleven in the Mint's collection of twelve for 1978 is a gold "Jack-in-the-Box" to hang on the Christmas tree.

"Snowflake III" (#12)

Registered at the Danbury Mint, in the name of the lucky subscribers is another golden "Snowflake III," the third and different one offered and the twelfth ornament issued in the "collection of twelve for 1978," created by Reed and Barton exclusively for this Mint. No ornament in this collection of three-dimensionals will ever be made available again.

── 11 ──
The Lincoln Mint Collection

The Lincoln Mint, located in Chicago, Illinois is noted worldwide for their medallion art commemorating the historical achievements of the United States and its people. Using the designs of famous artists and sculptors, they have issued ingots, medals, plates, and bells, singly and in collections, capturing great moments of the American way of life. In 1972, a great moment for the Lincoln Mint came about with their first issue of the Christmas Charmers ornament collection.

Christmas Charmers 1972

Heralding Angel—Star of Bethlehem—Choir Boys
Santa Claus—Christmas Tree—Shepherd

The Lincoln Mint introduced and made available a collection of six, limited-edition sterling-silver Christmas ornaments in 1972. This unique collection, designed exclusively for the Lincoln Mint by Colin Fry, delightfully captures important Christmas scenes. The magnificently detailed sculpturing is enhanced by a finish that is both brushed and polished. They were produced in "limited editions, hallmarked, serially numbered and registered and gift packaged." The issue price is $25.00.

"The Heralding Angel"

The "Heralding Angel" is an intricately detailed one, with a mop of curls, flying around, "Blowing Her Horn." Dimensions: 2″ h × 3″ w.

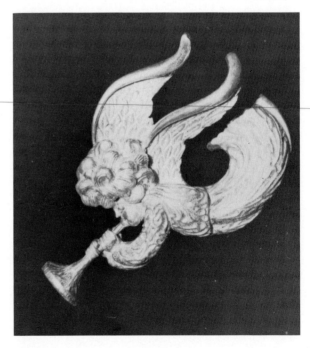

The Lincoln Mint's Heralding Angel–Holiday Charmers Collection 1972
PHOTO BY LINCOLN MINT

96

"Star of Bethlehem"

The legendary "Star of Bethlehem," with beams of light shining down on the stable and the countryside where Christ was born, is one of the six Christmas Charmers of the 1972 Lincoln Mint Collection. Dimensions 2¼″ h × 2¼″ w.

"Choir Boys"

Three adorable little "Choir Boys" wearing bangs, bows at the neck, and holding beautiful holiday songbooks are "caroling." Dimensions: 2¼″ h × 1¾″ w.

"Santa Claus"

Nothing is more charming than jolly old "Santa Claus" in his ornate sleigh, packed with "holiday trappings in gift wrappings" and on his way. Dimensions 2″ × 2″ w.

"Shepherd"

The star of Bethlehem beckons to a "Shepherd" as he brings a lamb back to the fold. Dimensions: 2½″ h × 2″ w.

"Christmas Tree"

O "Christmas Tree," O "Christmas Tree," you're glowing with eleven candles, topped with a star, and designed by Colin Fry for the Lincoln Mint in 1972. Dimensions 2¼″ h × 2⅛″ w.

The Lincoln Mint's Star of Bethlehem–Holiday Charmers Collection 1972
PHOTO BY LINCOLN MINT

The Lincoln Mint's Choir Boys   Holiday Charmers Collection 1972   PHOTO BY LINCOLN MINT

The Lincoln Mint's Santa Claus   Holiday Charmers Collection 1972   PHOTO BY LINCOLN MINT

*The Lincoln Mint's Shepherd   Holiday Charmers
Collection 1972*   PHOTO BY LINCOLN MINT

*The Lincoln Mint's Christmas Tree   Holiday Charmers
Collection 1972*   PHOTO BY LINCOLN MINT

12

The American Heritage Publishing Company, Inc. Collection

In 1947, the American Association for State and Local History, the national organization of U.S. state and city historians, began publishing a small, soft-covered, quarterly magazine named *American Heritage* to provide a medium for historians to reach the increasing number of general readers who were interested in American historical topics. In 1976, it was purchased by Engelhard Hanovia, a private investment company. At that time, Rhett Austell, a former vice-president of Time, Inc., was employed by Engelhard Hanovia to become the president and publisher.

Americana magazine was started to provide an attractive means to explore the practical, day-to-day uses of the American legacy. Its subjects range from antique collecting to traditional menus, from travel in search of history to class styles in houses, handcrafts, furnishings, and gardens. Every *Americana* presents a variety of such pleasures, occupations, and achievements from the past to admire, to emulate, to visit, and to enjoy. A number of these have been reproduced, in accurate replica, for sales through the annual "American Heritage Catalogue" and in other offers limited to its circle of readers.

Americana Ornament Collection

"Mt. Vernon Peace Dove" 1972

American Heritage commissioned the Gorham Company to produce an adaptation of the peace dove weathervane that George Washington installed at Mt. Vernon when he returned from the Revolutionary War. Four inches from olive branch to tail, this hollow, sterling "Mt. Vernon Peace Dove" ornament is light enough to hang gracefully from a tree, beautiful enough to grace a collector's shelves. Each piece is stamped with the American Heritage Society name, Gorham hallmark, and date. Issue price: $10.00.

Exclusive silver ornaments based on historical designs are created each year for American Heritage by the Gorham Company. They are no longer available. The first four "Collector's Ornaments" are adaptations of weather vanes.

"Christmas Reindeer" 1973

The second in the American Heritage annual series of Christmas ornaments with historical backgrounds is "Christmas Reindeer" 1973. This handsome tree decoration was inspired by an exceptionally fine American weathervane c. 1870. It is beautifully wrought in sterling silver by skilled craftsmen of the Gorham Company, with the date stamped on the back.

The "Christmas Reindeer" 1973 weighs one ounce and comes in a gift box. Dimensions: 3½″ h × 3¾″ w. Issue price: $15.00.

"Christmas Angel" 1974

The third in the American Heritage annual series of Christmas ornaments with historical backgrounds is "Christmas Angel" 1974. This handsome tree decoration was inspired by an exceptionally fine American weathervane made c. 1840. It is beautifully wrought in sterling silver by skilled craftsmen of the Gorham Company, with date stamped on back. The "Christmas Angel" 1974 weighs one ounce and comes in an attractive gift box. Dimensions: 4¼″ h × 2⅛″ w. Issue price: $20.00.

"Christmas Steam Engine" 1975

The fourth in the American Heritage series of Christmas ornaments is the "Steam Engine" 1975. Beautifully wrought by the Gorham Company of sterling silver, with the date stamped on the back. This handsome ornament was inspired by American Weathervane Designs of the mid-nineteenth century. Dimensions: 4½″ h × 2½″ w. Issue price: $20.00.

"St. Nicholas" 1976

The fifth in the American Heritage series of Christmas ornaments is "St. Nicholas" 1976. Beautifully wrought in sterling silver by the Gorham Company, it is a copy of one of the figures on a Victorian Christmas wreath, made by Mrs. Wanda Henry, fashioned from ornament designs of the 1890s. The date is stamped on the back. Dimensions: 2¼″ h × 3¾″ w. Issue price: $25.00.

"Children Round the Tree" 1977

The beautiful sterling-silver Christmas tree ornament was adapted from a Victorian design. It is the sixth annual collector's ornament created for American Heritage by the Gorham Company. The year is stamped on the back. Delivered in a handsome gift box. 1 oz. Dimensions: 2½″ h × 3⅝″ w. Issue price: $22.50.

The American Heritage Publishing Co.'s Collection
Christmas Reindeer 1973, Christmas Angel 1974,
Christmas Steam Engine 1974, St. Nicholas 1976,
Children "Round the Tree" 1977

The American Heritage Publishing Co.'s Collection
Santa In His Sleigh   *1978*

"Santa in His Sleigh" 1978

This beautiful sterling-silver Christmas tree ornament was adapted from a Victorian design. It is the seventh annual collector's ornament created for American Heritage by the Gorham Company. The year is stamped on the back. Delivered in a handsome gift box. Issue price: 25.00.

This collection is offered by mail to the subscribers of *American Heritage, Americana,* and *Horizon* publications, the publication donors, and outside lists in September of each year. With the exception of the "First," this collection is still available, as of 1978. The collection is expected to continue with an "Americana" offering in 1979. Issue price: $25.00.

The Metropolitan Museum of Art's 1976 Snowflake

The Metropolitan Museum of Art's 1978 Snowflake

The Metropolitan Museum of Art's 1977 Snowflake

"Snowflake" 1978
(eighth edition)

The 1978 "Snowflake," designed by Linae Frei, is the eighth in an annual series by contemporary artists. Created in sterling or sterling on copper with a ring at the top, this "Snowflake" is a beautiful addition to this Christmas ornament collection. In special box with descriptive text. Diameter: 3⅛". Issue price: sterling silver on copper, $9.75; sterling silver, $22.50. This collection will continue.

"Snowflake" 1979
(ninth edition)

A sparkling "Snowflake," designed by Lance Hioy, is the ninth annual edition offered by the Metropolitan Museum of Art. Diameter: 3¼". Issue price: sterling silver, $28.50; silver on copper, $11.50.

*The Metropolitan Museum of Art's 1972 First Annual
Star*

Stars

"Star" 1972
(first edition in gold)

A star in gold for a Christmas tree
—or a Christmas wreath
—or to mix with holly
—or to hang with mistletoe
—or to float in solitary splendor
A magnificent Christmas ornament, a sterling
"Star" surfaced in pure gold and was designed
by Jozef Domjan. It was made available through
the mail or at the gift shop of the Metropolitan
Museum of Art, New York City, for the 1972
Christmas season. This beautiful "Star" marked
the beginning of treasured, annual collections to
be designed by contemporary artists and issued
annually. Diameter: 3⅛". Issue price: $12.50.
No longer available.

"Star" 1973
(second edition)

An interpretation of the Christmas star by Fritz Kredel is a galaxy of golden crescent moons and "Stars" encompassed within a greater "Star." Wrought in sterling silver and surfaced with pure gold, it is second in an annual series of "Stars" by contemporary artists. The year 1973 is marked on reverse and a ring is at top for hanging. Diameter: 3⅛". Each "Star" in this collection comes in special box with descriptive text. Issue price: $12.50. No longer available.

"Star" 1974
(third edition)

Jozef Domjan created his interpretation of the Christmas "Star" in 1974. The third in an annual series of stars by contemporary artists has the year marked on reverse and has a ring at top for hanging from a pine bough or wherever you wish. Diameter: 3⅛". Issue prices: pure gold on copper, $9.50; pure gold on sterling silver, $18.50. No longer available.

"Star" 1975
(fourth edition)

The fourth in an annual series of "Stars" by contemporary artists was created by Lance Hidy. It is dated 1975 and is ready to take its place among the "Stars." Diameter: 3⅛". Issue prices: pure gold on copper, $9.75; pure gold on sterling silver, $22.50. No longer available.

"Star" 1976
(fifth edition)

An interpretation of the "Trilogy" sometimes called the Christmas "Star" by Tia Stoller, is the fifth in an annual series for the Metropolitan Museum by contemporary artists. It is ringed at the top for hanging and dated 1976 on the back. Diameter: 3⅛". Issue prices: 24 k gold plate on copper, $9.75; 24 k gold plate on sterling silver, $22.50. No longer available.

The Metropolitan Museum of Art's 1973 Second Annual Star

"Star" 1977
(sixth edition)

In 1977 an interpretation of the Christmas "Star" was designed by Sundra Mayer. The sixth in an annual series is dated on the back and is a brilliant addition to the "Star" collection. Diameter: 3⅛". 24 k gold electroplate on copper, $9.75: issue price. 24 k gold electroplate on sterling silver: $22.50, issue price. No longer available.

"Star" 1978
(seventh edition)

The sparkling Christmas "Star" of 1978 is Linae Frei's interpretation. This seventh in an annual series by contemporary artists is another golden creation in the "Star" collection from the Metropolitan Museum of Art. Diameter: 3⅛". In special box with descriptive text. 24 k gold electroplate on copper, $9.75: issue price. 24 k gold electroplate on sterling silver, $22.50: issue price. This collection will continue.

The Metropolitan Museum of Art's 1974 Third Annual Star

The Metropolitan Museum of Art's 1975 Fourth Annual Star

The Metropolitan Museum of Art's 1976 Fifth Annual Star

"Star" 1979
(eighth edition)

An interpretation of the Christmas "Star," by Elizabeth Hyder, is the eighth in an annual series for 1979 designed by contemporary artists. Diameter: 3¼". Issue prices: 24 kt gold on sterling silver, $28.50; 24 kt gold on copper, $11.50.

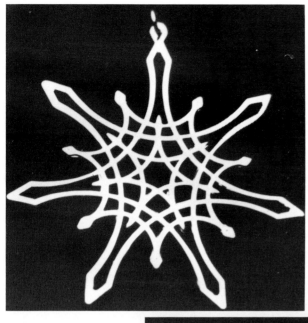

The Metropolitan Museum of Arts 1977 Sixth Annual Star

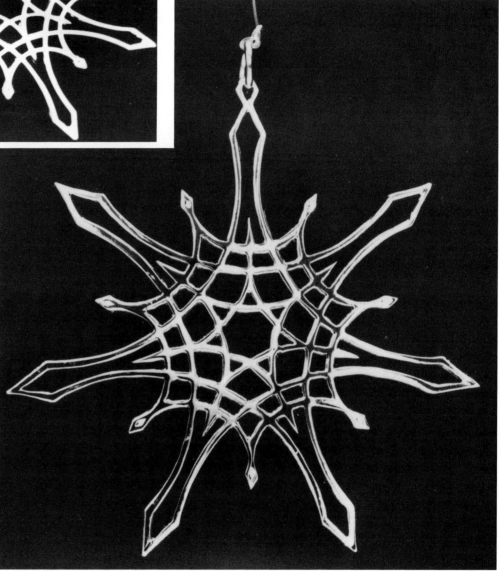

The Metropolitan Museum of Art's 1978 Seventh Annual Star

The Metropolitan Museum of Art's 1978 Sixth Annual Star

Christmas Bell Collection

"Christ Crib Bell" 1973

The first edition of tiny bells, 1973, one in pure silver and one in pure gold are copies of decorations from a rare fifteenth century miniature of a jeweled crib for the Christ Child. These small bells have a sweet and individual sound when rung. They may be tied with ribbons from the tips of Christmas tree boughs or used in countless different ways. Each in a special box with descriptive text. Issue price: sterling silver, $7.50; 14 k gold, $25.00.

"Furin Bell" 1974

The gentlest wind will swing the elegant clapper of this bell and sound a sweet silver note. This "Furin," or "wind bell," was often made in sets of four, and the individual bells were suspended at the four corners of the eaves of a temple. This smaller version makes a delightful ornament or a shining addition to a Christmas tree from the Museum's Crosby Brown Collection of Musical Instruments. It is of Japanese origin and dates from the nineteenth century or earlier. Dimension: 2½" h. Issue price; sterling silver, $18.50.

"Katerina Bell" 1975

In 1975, the museum made available a miniature version of the bell "Katerina," one of the largest bells at the Benedictine Cloister of St. Peter at Naestved, Denmark. It was made by Martinus, the Master of the Calendarum Naestwedense, and is thought to have been cast between 1270–80. The original is decorated with a design which depicts Martinus presenting the bell to St. Peter. It makes a delightful ornament or a shining addition to a Christmas tree.

*There was no bell issued in 1976.

"Beehive Bell" 1977

The 1977 fourth edition, small beehive-shaped bell from the Museum's Crosby Brown Collection of Musical Instruments may have once decorated a Christmas tree in nineteenth century Russia, "the land of bells." Today it can shine from among pine branches or sweetly summon one and all to a festive dinner. Dimension: 2¾" h. Issue price: sterling silver, $35.00.

"Bird Bells" 1978

Issued in 1978, two versions of jaunty little birds perched atop bells, are originally from Costa Rica, eleven to fifteenth century. Ornamental and delightful, they may be worn around the neck, as they were centuries ago, or incorporated with holiday greenery as a particularly festive decoration. The bells have a clear, delicate ring. Available in sterling silver, with 24 k gold electroplate. Issue price: $24.00 each.

"Christ Crib Bells" 1979

The "Christ Crib Bell" originally issued in 1974, at $7.50 in sterling silver and $22.50 in 14 kt. gold, was re-issued in 1979. Issue prices: sterling, $22.50; 14 kt. gold, $95.00.

The "Furin" Bell of 1974 reappeared in 1979, at $39.50.

The Metropolitan Museum of Art's 1978 Fifth Annual
Bell Collection

"Tree-Top Ornament"

A galaxy of golden, crescent moons and stars
to glisten from a tree top. Wrought in copper,
surfaced with 24 kt gold and made available in
1979 by the Metropolitan Museum of Art. A
fixture on the reverse allows the star to be attached to a tree top. Designer: Fritz Dredel.
Diameter: 6″. Issue price: $18.75.

113

—— *14* ——

The Smithsonian Collections

Made by Stieff

By an act of Congress, approved on August 10, 1846, the Smithsonian Institution was established. James Smithson, born in France in 1765, the illegitimate son of Sir Hugh Percy (nee Smithson), first Duke of Northumberland, and Elizabeth Keate Macie, a wealthy widow and heiress of the Hungerfords of Studley, was educated in and became a naturalized citizen of England. Mr. Smithson lived a very comfortable life, traveled the world over pursuing his hobbies and gambling, and was a renowned scientist with twenty-seven published scientific papers to his credits. He died on June 27, 1829, leaving a will bequeathing $508,318,460, "to the United States of America, to found at Washington, under the name of the Smithsonian Institution, an establishment for the increase and diffusion of knowledge among men." He stated in his will that this was to be done if, his nephew, the Baron Eunice de La Batut, died without heirs, which indeed is what occurred six years later.

The Stieff Company, founded in 1892 as the Baltimore Silver Co. by Charles C. Stieff, is known worldwide for their fine sterling flatware and holloware. They are the exclusive manufacturers of Williamsburg, Newport, and Old Sturbridge village sterling silver and pewter reproductions and were chosen by the Smithsonian to reproduce in sterling silver, objects and items from the worldwide collections housed at the Smithsonian.

The Gabriel Angel

A familiar sight in America, the latter part of the nineteenth century, was the weathervane, atop houses and other buildings, determining wind direction. The Archangel Gabriel, a thirty-two-inch-long weather vane made and copyrighted in 1883 by L. W. Cushing & Sons of Waltham, Maine, now housed in the Smithsonian, was chosen to be reproduced in sterling silver as a Christmas ornament by Stieff. The 4⅞" long ornament first offered in 1972 is subscribed to through the Smithsonian catalog, is unlimited, and its issue price was $24.75 to Smithsonian members and $27.50 to non-members. Dimensions: 5" h x 1¾" w.

The Smithsonian Institute's Gabriel Angel
PHOTO BY STIEFF SILVER CO.

The Ethiopian Ceremonial Bell

An adaptation of an ancient "Ethiopian Ceremonial Bell" collected in Addis Ababa in 1909, now in the permanent collection of the Smithsonian, was the second ornament produced by Stieff and issued in 1973 by the Smithsonian, in heavy sterling. It is a beautiful, small, classic, and simple ornament, issued in a brown-and-white presentation case with two leather straps, one long and black, and the other, short and red, to be used on the tree or worn around the neck. Each issue is and will be a reflection of the past and a reproduction of an artifact of the Smithsonian's collections. Each will bear the imprint of the institution's well-known castle. This collection will eventually be a beautiful collection of worldwide artifacts to enjoy in your own home. Dimensions: 2" h. Issue price: $29.75.

The Smithsonian Institute's Ethiopian Coptic Cross
PHOTO BY STIEFF SILVER CO.

Ethiopian Coptic Cross

One of the Smithsonian's baubles to dangle from bright, shiny trees is their "Coptic Cross" pendant/ornament. The deep-sculptured, sterling-silver relief, classic cross is a round heavy medallion designed with the "Coptic Cross," an artifacts to enjoy in your own home. Dimension: at the Smithsonian in Washington, D.C. It dates from the fourth century when Ethiopia converted to Christianity. Diameter: 2½". Issue price: $29.50.

The Smithsonian Institute's Ethiopian Ceremonial Bell
PHOTO BY STIEFF SILVER CO.

Weathervane Collection

"Triton" 1978

In 1978 the staff at the Smithsonian chose from its collection of worldwide priceless objects and artifacts, an early New England weathervane called a "Triton" ("Triton" was a legendary Greek diety who had the ability to arouse or calm the ocean by simply blowing his horn) to be adapted in miniature, as a Christmas ornament by designer, José Barata, at Stieff. This "Triton" ornament looks like a "curled tailed mermaid" blowing a horn and is adapted in sterling silver with "Christmas 1978" engraved on the body. It is the "first edition" of an annual collection from the Smithsonian Institution. Dimensions: 2¼″ h x 3¼″ w. Issue price: $14.95. No issue for 1979.

The Smithsonian Institute's "Triton" 1978 First Edition
PHOTO BY STIEFF SILVER CO.

The Smithsonian Institute's Gabriel Angel   Ethiopian Ceremonial Bell and the Ethiopian Coptic Cross
PHOTO BY STIEFF SILVER CO.

15

Oneida Silversmiths Collections

"Heirloom Edition" Reindeer (Flatware)
"Heirloom Edition" Christmas Religious Series
Oneida's "Tree Trimmer" Collections (Holloware Div.)
General Mills "Dimensional Tree Trimmers" by Oneida

In the year 1877, in a commune at Oneida Creek, New York, John Humphrey Noyes and an association of men started the "Oneida Community" company, makers of tableware. The company became the Oneida-Silversmiths in 1926, producers of fine silverplated holloware. In 1973, Oneida began producing beautiful sterling Christmas ornaments. I often wondered why they were called "Community Plate," now I know.

Designer of "JOY," "NATIVITY," "MAGI," "CUPID," and "VIXEN" are Oneida Ltd. Design Studios, Frank Perry, director. Christmas ornaments—staff design. Designers: Ellen Manderfield, Melvin Lea and John Czasonis.

Oneida Silversmith's Joy 1973 First of the Religious Series, Heirloom Collection PHOTO BY ONEIDA

"Joy to the World" Christmas Religious Series
1973

Heirloom Edition (Sterling)

Oneida Silversmiths presented in 1973, the first of their annual "Heirloom Edition" Christmas religious series ornament called "Joy to the World." The front of the ovate, sterling medallion portrays in three-dimension, an angel triumphantly heralding the holiday season. Depicted on the back is a stylized star symbolizing the star of Bethlehem. 11,474 were issued. Dimensions: 3″ h x 2¼″ w.

Oneida Silversmith's Nativity 1974 Religious Series,
Heirloom Collection PHOTO BY ONEIDA

"The Nativity" 1974

The "Nativity," crafted in exquisite detail of
sterling and vermeil was a 1974 member of
Oneida's "Heirloom Edition" collection. It depicts the birth of the infant Jesus. Within a frame
of sterling silver, the joy of this sacred season is
portrayed in gold electroplate, Mary and Joseph
looking lovingly at their newborn son. Dated and
hallmarked on the back. Only 7,188 were produced and will never be repeated. Diameter:
2". Issue price: $10.00.

Oneida Silversmith's Magi 1975 Religious Series
Heirloom Collection PHOTO BY ONEIDA

"The Magi" 1975

Within a gleaming oval sterling frame, the three wise men, Melchoir, Balthasar, and Gaspar are exquisitely depicted with their precious gifts of gold, frankincense, and myrrh to lay at the feet of the Christ Child. In the background of "The Magi" can be seen a star shining above the little town of Bethlehem. The 1975 "Magi" is a cherished memento of the holiday and the last of the Oneida "Heirloom Edition" Christmas religious series collection planned at this writing. Only 1,974 were made and are never to be repeated. They are dated, limited, and hallmarked.Diameter: 2″. Issue price: $27.50. Collection closed.

Oneida Silversmith's Heirloom Collection Cupid 1974
PHOTO BY ONEIDA

"Cupid" Santa's Reindeer 1974

Heirloom Edition Reindeer

One of the happiest fantasies of childhood is
Santa's eight tiny reindeer. Oneida craftsmen
help to re-create childhood happy memories by
introducing as a part of their "Heirloom Edition" collection in 1974, a tiny, sterling-silver
"Cupid" as the first of a planned series for the
coming year. The handsome, prancing "Cupid"
is antlered, and his name is embossed in his very
ornate saddle. The ornament bears Oneida's
hallmark and the date on the back and can be
worn as a pin. Only 7,589 were produced and will
never be repeated. Dimensions: 2¼" l ×
2⅞" w. Issue price: $17.00.

121

Oneida Silversmith's Heirloom Collection Vixen 1975
PHOTO BY ONEIDA

"Vixen" Santa's Reindeer 1975

The second and unfortunately, I have been told by Oneida, the last of Santa's reindeer was issued in the 1975 "Heirloom Edition" collection. Spunky little "Vixen" managed to sneak off the drawing board and through the production lines before "Scrooge Oneida" shut down on Santa's reindeer, aborting Dasher, Dancer, Prancer, Donder and Blitzen, Coment and Rudolph. Cruel, cruel! "Vixen" dons a beautiful saddle designed with his name and roses and scrolling on his body beautiful! He and "Cupid" are fated by Oneida to pull Santa's sleigh, alone, in the dark, forever! Limited to 2,485, dated and hallmarked and never to be repeated. Dimensions: 2 1/5″ h x 2 1/5″ w. Issue price: $15.00.

No. 9602 MADONNA   No. 9606 POINSETTIA   No. 9607 HOLLY

No. 9608 NOEL   No. 9609 REINDEER   No. 9605 SLEIGH

Oneida Silversmith's 1977 Tree Trimmers
PHOTO BY ONEIDA

Tree Trimmer Collections 1977

Sparkling, silver-plated and gold-electroplated Tree Trimmers in a choice of eighteen shimmering designs in three collections were placed on the market by Oneida in 1977. The unlimited, undated ornaments are detailed in many Christmas motifs and are coated to resist tarnish.

Silver-Plated Flat Tree Trimmers 1977

The six flat, 2½″ diameter Tree Trimmers were issued at $2.50 each and the cut-out designs are called "Madonna," "Poinsettia," "Holly," "Noel," "Reindeer" and "Sleigh."

123

No. 9651 JOY   No. 9653 ANGEL   No. 9654 CANDLE

No. 9655 PARTRIDGE IN PEAR TREE   No. 9652 SLEIGH   No. 9656 SNOWFLAKE

Oneida Silversmith's Dimensional Tree Trimmers 1977
PHOTO BY ONEIDA

Silver and Gold Electroplate Dimensionals 1977

The 2½″ six-dimensionals were issued at $5.95 each. A "bowl"- or "concave"-shaped disc in silver plate holds an intricate, gold-plated, flat disc that gives a mirrored reflection to sparkle on the tree. The "dimensionals" are called "Sleigh," "Snowflake," "Candle," "Partridge in a Pear Tree," "Angel" and "Joy."

No. 9611 CHRISTMAS TREE   No. 9604 BELL   No. 9610 ANGEL WITH TRUMPET

No. 9600 SANTA WITH PACK   No. 9603 DOVE   No. 9601 SNOWFLAKE

Oneida Silversmith's 1977 Mobile Tree Trimmers

The Mobiles 1977

Issued in six designs, the Mobiles are designed to "twirl" and turn within their silver plated circles, constantly sparkling, shining, and reflecting the lights of the tree. Issue price is $2.50 each; issue size, 2¼″. Issue names and/or designs are "Dove," "Bell," "Snowflake," "Santa with Pack," "Angel with Trumpet" and "Christmas Tree."

Silver Trimmers 1978

Oneida in 1978 created a collection of twenty designs of silver and gold electroplated Christmas ornaments for the 1978 holiday season, called "Spherical" (2), "Interlocking" (2), "Teardrops" (6), "Mobiles" (6), and "Trimmers" (4) in price ranges for any and all, to create a sparkling tree.

125

Spherical "Wreath"

Two "Wreaths," in silver and gold electroplate, are connected, lacey stampings, topped with a large bow. A lovely reflective ornament offered by Oneida in 1978 at $9.95. 2¾ × 2½".

Spherical "Holly"

Oneida's "Spherical Holly" is designed in a wreath fashion, has holly leaves and berries, and a bow at the top. It is a 3" high by 2½" wide double, electroplated ornament in silver and gold. Issue price: $9.95.

"Interlocking" Ornaments

The two "Interlocking" ornaments are just that, two electroplated gold and silver stampings interlocking to form a three-dimensional look of frills and lace and issued at $5.95 each.
1. A "Bell," hanging in the center of a Victorian-type wreath.
2. A pear has a center design of a "Partridge."

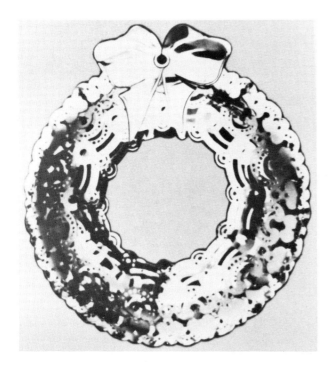

Oneida Silversmith's Spherical Wreath 1978
PHOTO BY ONEIDA

Oneida Silversmith's Spherical Bell 1978
PHOTO BY ONEIDA

Oneida Silversmith's Spherical Holly 1978
PHOTO BY ONEIDA

Oneida Silversmith's Spherical Peas 1978
PHOTO BY ONEIDA

Oneida Silversmith's Tree Trimmers Collection 1978
PHOTO BY ONEIDA

"Trimmers"

"Noel," "Madonna," and the "Reindeer," introduced in 1977, return in 1978, bringing "Santa" with them. Santa appears to be bending over to put a sled under the tree. Dimension: 2½" h each. Issue price: $2.50 each.

"Mobiles"

The 1978 six "Mobiles" came in various shapes, but all were silver-plated and cost $2.50 each. They were designed with an outer rim and an inner designed flat open-work ornament to be connected by a card so that the inner ornament could form the "Mobile."

1. "Christmas Tree," in a circle, 2½" × 2½", decorated with a base.
2. The shape of the figure "Santa" with his backpack of gifts in a 2½" circle.
3. Stamped out "Dove" with an olive branch in his beak in a 2½" circle.
4. Teardrop-shaped rim holding an oblong, lacey "Christmas Ball." 3½" high.
5. A "Christmas Bird" hangs in the center of a slightly squared, ornate frame with a plate at the base that can be engraved. 3½" high.
6. A harp-playing "Angel" twirls from the center of a six-pointed rim. Diameter: 2½".

Oneida Silversmith's Mobile Tree Trimmers 1978

9603 DOVE

9611 CHRISTMAS TREE

9600 SANTA

9618 ANGEL

9617 CHRISTMAS BALL

9619 CHRISTMAS BIRD

129

9662 CROWN

9651 JOY

9660 MADONNA TEARDROP

9655 PARTRIDGE

9625 STAR

9626 CANDLE

Oneida Silversmith's Teardrop Tree Trimmers 1978

130

General Mills 1977 Collection of Dimensional Tree Trim-mers
PHOTO BY KEVIN NASH

"Teardrops"

A collection of six "Teardrops" ornaments, in silver and gold electroplate were issued by Oneida in 1978 at $5.95 each. Each ornament is 3½″ high by 2½″ wide and has a silver-plated back that holds the electroplated gold, stamped-out ornament inset. They are called:

1. "Star"
2. "Partridge"
3. "Crown"
4. "Madonna"
5. "Candle"
6. "Joy"

General Mills Dimensional Tree Trimmers
Collection
by Oneida

General Mills, Inc. of Minneapolis, the "food" company, got the "Spirit" of Christmas and in on the "act" in 1977 with "Christmas Ornaments." Their collection of eight "limited and dated" silver and gold electroplated ornaments made by Oneida were offered through mail from adver-tising in national magazines. They are beautiful and similar to Oneida's "dimensional" orna-ments, and according to my checkbook, issue price with postage was $18.90 for the eight.

131

General Mills 1978 Dimensional Collection

The names of the 2½″ ornaments are "Poinsettia," "Angel with Horn," "Candles," "Snowflake," "Madonna and Chld," "Dove," and "Christmas Tree." This is a lovely little collection, reasonable in price, and a lasting memento of the 1977 Christmas season.

Tree Trimmer Collection by Oneida Silversmiths 1978
PHOTO BY ONEIDA

— 16 —
The Cazenovia Abroad Ltd. Collection

Pat and John Trush founded a gift store of "Distinctive imports for Discerning Americans" in 1967 in Cazenovia, New York and named it "Cazenovia Abroad, Ltd."

After traveling with her husband John through Europe on sales business, Pat thought it would be fun to import some of the beautiful European wares she had seen and open a gift shop. One of her "sterling ideas" was making available to Americans, silver Christmas tree ornaments, made in Portugal by Topazio or the firm Ferrira Marques and Irmao founded in 1875. Thus, sterling-silver tree decorations, to become a part of "The Heritage of Americans" were offered beginning with the 1968 holiday season.

In the manner of old world craftsmanship, much of the work of these ornaments is hand done in a long, tedious process. First sold only in Cazenovia to the local people, this collection became so popular that Pat Thrush began distributing to firms such as Marshall Field (Chicago), Shreve, Crump and Low of Boston, Caldwell in Philadelphia, Henri Bendell in New York, and Joseph Magnin in San Francisco. Now they are distributed by Pat on a nationwide basis and can be found in most quality jewelers and department stores.

These ornaments are all sterling silver, three-dimensional and some are copyrighted. Those with copyright are marked with a circled "C" (C),

copyright date and R. M. Trush. The "standing" and the "tiptoe" angels are patented but are marked only with "sterling" and "Portugal." Pat designs many and calls on the artisians at Topazio to assist.

Offering to date and issue prices are:

"Dove of Peace"—$20.00
"Bunny"—$20.00
"Teddy Bear"—$20.00
"Porky Pig"—$20.00
"Tiptoe Angel"—$20.00
"Kneeling Angel"—$34.50
"Standing Angel"—$26.50
"Tree Top Angel"—$22.50
"Large Bird Songster"—$20.00
"Fawn"—$20.00
"Snowman Caroler"—$20.00
"Toy Soldier"—$25.00
"Elephant"—$20.00
"Duck"—$20.00
"Cat"—$20.00
"Rooster"—$20.00
"Hatching Chick"—$24.00
"Rocking Horse"—$34.50
"Star"—$20.00
"Owl"—$24.00
"Donkey"—$25.00
"Conch Shell"—$24.00
"Raggedy Ann"—$30.00

Cazenovia Abroad Ltd. Collection

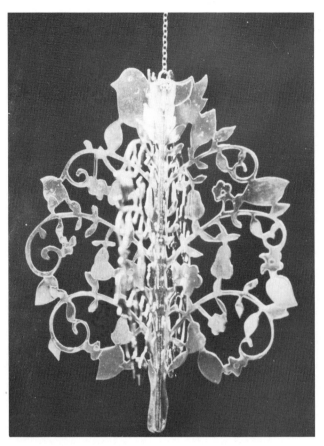

John John Enterprises First Day of the Twelve Days of Christmas
PHOTO BY KEVIN NASH

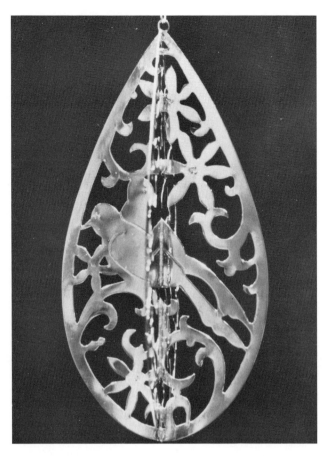

John John Enterprises Second Day of Christmas
PHOTO BY KEVIN NASH

stamped with the company's Bell hallmark.

Even though it was not widely distributed and not many were made, this ornament is still available. Dimensions: 3¾" h x 2" w. Issue price: $25.00.

"Two Turtle Doves"
(1976—second edition)

"Two Turtle Doves," 1976, are shown "billing and cooing" on a branch in the center of this three-dimensional sterling ornament. It is in a tear-drop shape and "cut-out" to show branches, leaves, and flowers around the "Doves." It has a sterling hook attached, is marked sterling, and is stamped with the Bell hallmark. Designer: James Glisson. Dimensions: 4½" h x 1¾" w. Issue price: $25.00.

"Three French Hens"
(1978—third edition)

Snowflake 1975

A twelve-pointed, lacy, modern "Snowflake" in three dimensions by John-John designers was issued in 1975. Each of the twelve points has five points and the center is a cut-out "Snowflake" with the feeling of a wheel with six spokes. It's a frosty looking beauty! It is available, unlimited, sterling, and hallmarked. Dimensions: 3" h × 2¾" w. Issue price: $20.00.

141

Holly Sprig 1974

If I were rich, this unique "Holly Sprig" ornament would be a part of all my decorative gift wrapping at Christmas time. Since I am not, this 1974 design of Joseph Parker dons my tree for all to see. Just imagine two actual holly leaves in brushed sterling showing their sharp prickley points, attached at the stems with three polished sterling, individual holly berries, hanging on your tree! The design department is extremely imaginative and production runs are small at this company, but a limited number of their ornaments are available. The "Holly Sprig" is hallmarked. Dimensions: 3½″ h × 3″ w. Issue price: $20.00

Not any of the John-John ornaments are dated of "limited edition" nor are they available from most dealers, department stores, or jewelers.

Holly Bell 1975

Traditional holly designs of leaves and berries bordering a sterling "Holly Bell" with gold wash inside was created at John-John by their design department in 1975. The open bell is stamped on the top with the Bell hallmark of John–John and is marked starling. It is available at all stores carrying John/products. It is not limited or dated. Dimensions: 2½″ h × 2⅝″ w. Issue price: $25.00.

Christmas Star 1975

James Glisson's interpretation of the star of Bethlehem was created in sterling for John-John in 1975. The ten-pointed, three-dimensional star called the "Christmas Star" gives the effect of tremendous brilliance by its many-faceted, center cut-out designs. It is hallmarked, marked sterling, unlimited, and available. Dimension: 3″ h. Issue price: $20.00.

John John's 1975 Snowflake
PHOTO BY KEVIN NASH

John John's 1974 Holly Sprig
PHOTO BY KEVIN NASH

John John's 1975 Holly Bell
PHOTO BY KEVIN NASH

John John's 1976 Reindeer
PHOTO BY KEVIN NASH

Reindeer 1976

One of Santa's "Reindeer," with two antlers and many points, was made by John-John in 1976. It is a 4″ tall, tear-drop ornament in John-John's popular three-dimensional, cut-out design. The curly, lacey, open-work execution of the ornament gives the feeling that the "Reindeer" is standing in his natural habitat, the forest. It is marked "sterling" and is hallmarked by John-John. This "Reindeer" is available. Issue price: $35.00.

Treetopper 1978

To top off a tree of sterling silver, limited and annual Christmas ornaments, nothing will do except a sterling silver or silver-plated, limited-edition "Treetopper." John-John Enterprises, manufacturer, and James Parker, designer, filled that need in 1978 with a classic versatile star. A versatile ornament, the "Treetopper" can

The John John Enterprises Collection
PHOTO BY JOHN JOHN ENTERPRISES

be used standing on a table, hanging as an ornament, or with its stand, topping the tree. The three-dimensional sterling star has a small sterling bell hanging in its center opening that can be removed to be used as an ornament alone. The "Treetopper" has its own sterling removable hook used for hanging on the tree. It is quality in design, sterling weight, and versatile. It can be secured from all dealers of John – John Enterprises Products. These beautiful ornaments are difficult to get. Dimensions: 4¾″ h x 4″ w. Issue price: $50.00.

___ 19 ___
Collections by John-John Enterprises (Inman) for Department Stores and Jewelers

Divisions:

Caldwells, Philadelphia, Pennsylvania
J. B. Hudsons, Minneapolis, Minnesota
J. Jessops & Sons, San Diego, California
Shreve, San Francisco, California
Charles W. Warren, Detroit, Michigan
Peacocks, Chicago, Illinois
Halls, Kansas City, Missouri
Lord & Taylor—New York, New York
Horchow's
Dayton Hudson Jewelers

Lord and Taylor Department Store

"Christmas Bell" 1977

"First Christmas" engraved on a sterling-silver, open bell with three ridges bordering the bottom was made by John-John in 1977 for Lord and Taylor exclusively. It is 2½″ high, gold washed on the inside, marked "Lord and Taylor" and "Sterling" on the top. It was reissued in 1978 and sold in the children's department of the store. Issue price: $25.00.

Lord and Taylor Department Store's "First Christmas" Bell
PHOTO BY KEVIN NASH

"Trifles"

Horchow Collections

Roger Horchow and his wife Carolyn, through a combination of creativity, genius, and a wealth of experience in the field, have become the royalty of the catalog mail-order business. The former vice-president of the mail-order department of Neiman-Marcus purchased his own mail-order business (The Kenton Catalog) and renamed it "The Horchow Collection" in 1973. The business sales zoomed like a rocket and went from a million dollar deficit to now grossing 20 million dollars annually.

This catalog, the answer to a prayer for the unusual gifts, does its greatest business at Christmastime, with shoppers from the affluent, movie stars, and royalty to the "trendy" and housewife. In 1978 another catalog, "Trifles," grew out of this Dallas, Texas, based company, headed by Bess DuVal as director (also formerly of Neiman-Marcus) who designed a Christmas ornament to be made available only through "Trifles." "Trifles" is a beautiful sterling-silver trinket for the universal Christmas tree. Made available for the first time in 1978 through the catalog by the same name, the ornament is tear-drop shaped and engraved "Christmas 1978." It is the beginning of an annual issue and at present, plans are that no change in *design* will be made from year to year except the *date* of engraving. It is made by John-John, designed by Bess DuVal, has its own sterling hook for hanging, and is marked "Sterling" and "Trifles." Diameter: 2½" h. Issue price: $25.00.

Horchow's 1978 First Edition "Trifles"
PHOTO BY HORCHOW

Dayton Hudson Jewelers

Dayton Hudson Jewelers was created in 1969 with the merger of two retailing giants, the Dayton Company of Minneapolis and the J. L. Hudson Company of Detroit. The merger brought together Charles W. Warren Jewelers of Detroit in 1965, Shreve's of San Francisco in 1967, Caldwell's of Philadelphia and Peacock's of Chicago in 1969, and Jessop's of San Diego in 1970.

All of these divisions were originally independent, family-owned businesses. They are leading guild jewelers in their respective cities, with long-established reputations for excellence. The joint effort of the six divisions as Dayton Hudson Jewelers has made them one of the most powerful influences in the jewelry business today, even though each has retained its prestige and individual identity.

J. E. Caldwell (Division of Dayton Hudson)

The founder, James E. Caldwell, first opened his Philadelphia store with an assortment of fine watches, fashionable jewelry, English and French fancy goods and silver-ware, plus custom designs made to order. During its first thirty years, Caldwell's was located on Philadelphia's fashionable Chestnut St. In 1869, the building was totally destroyed in an explosion. However, many valuable items were kept in fireproof safes, making it possible for business to resume at the same address shortly thereafter.

Under the leadership of J. Albert Caldwell, who succeeded his father in 1881, Caldwell's supplied numerous presentation silver services to the U.S. Navy. In 1897, Caldwell's designed a commemorative silver vase which was presented to King Oscar of Sweden.

J. Albert Caldwell was succeeded in 1914 by his son, J. Emmet Caldwell, who, in 1916, moved the store to its present downtown Philadelphia location at Chestnut and Juniper Streets.

J. B. Hudson (Division of Dayton Hudson)

In 1885, Minneapolis, the bustling commercial hub of the entire Northwest, was a city characterized by the prosperity of its citizens. Josiah B. Hudson found the city an ideal place for a dealer in fine jewelry to cater to the tastes and incomes of its wealthy millers, lumber barons, and financiers.

In 1911, Mr. Hudson's son joined him in the successful business. James B. Dougherty took over the leadership of J.B. Hudson Jewelers in 1922 and continued until 1951.

Hudson's retained its name and prestigious identity when, in 1929, it became the "crown jewel" of Dayton's department store at Nicollet Mall, Minneapolis.

As part of its seventy-fifth anniversary celebration in 1960, Hudson's displayed the famous Crown of the Andes, made in Columbia, South America, in 1599, containing 435 emeralds.

Jessop's (Division of Dayton Hudson)

Joseph Jessop founded this family-owned business in England in 1860 and, in 1893, moved the firm to San Diego. Family members are still active in the business, with the fourth and fifth generations currently participating in the ad-

ministration and operation of the company.

Jessop's famous street clock, a San Diego landmark, standing in front of Jessop's main store, was created by the Jessop's in 1907. The twenty dials on the clock tell the hour, minute, second, month, date and day of the week, as well as the time of day in twelve of the world's principal cities. Jewels for the clock are native to San Diego. The Jessops themselves mined and cut the tourmaline, jade, topaz, and agate. Every part of the intricate mechanism was designed and crafted by hand in the Jessop's shop.

Jessop's first branch store in La Jolla, opened in 1949, is the oldest branch store in the Dayton Hudson Jewelers' chain.

Shreve & Co. (Division of Dayton Hudson)

Shreve & Company, a San Francisco institution since Gold Rush days, is the foremost jeweler of California and the west. Founded by brothers George C. and S. S. Shreve, the firm was part of the early growth of the city.

The store moved to its present address at Post St. and Grant Ave. for the first time in 1892, and, for the second time, two years after the store was destroyed in the San Francisco fire of 1912.

Shreve's manufactured much of its own silverware until 1970 when the Towle Silversmith Company took over production of the exclusive Shreve patterns.

Over the years Shreve's has exhibited many priceless items in its stores. Among the exhibits have been the fabulous Crown of the Andes with its 435 emeralds, the uncut 726-carat Younkers Diamond, the jewels of Russia's Catherine the Great, and the exquisitely carved, polished, sapphire heads of Lincoln and Eisenhower.

Shreve's has also made and sold such unusual items as an 18-carat gold, life-size rooster, a 14-carat gold, 10-inch high Statute of Liberty for the wife of a foreign president, gifts for delegates to the founding of the United Nations, and the state of California's coronation gift to Queen Elizabeth II.

Charles W. Warren (Division of Dayton Hudson)

The original small store founded by partners Charles W. Warren and Frank R. Fitch, located in Detroit's Washington Arcade, carried only jewelry and household silver. However, a full range of merchandise, as well as a reputation for high standards of quality and workmanship, accompanied the C. W. Warren Company, as it is known, in its 1952 move to a new location on Washington Blvd.

The C. W. Warren Company was purchased in June 1965, by the J. L. Hudson Company of Detroit. Therefore, Warren's became a subsidiary of Dayton Hudson Jewelers when Hudson's merged with the Dayton Company of Minneapolis in 1969.

C. W. Warren has long been famous for its magnificent collection of porcelain birds created by Edward Marshall Boehm.

C. D. Peacock (Division of Dayton Hudson)

Elijah Peacock came from London, England, to the village of Chicago in 1837 and opened a small service-oriented jewelry shop specializing in clock repair and the adjustment of chronometers for the sailing boats on Lake Michigan. In 1860, when his son, Charles Daniel Peacock became sole owner of the store, the selection of merchandise had expanded to include fine jewelry, watches, silver, and fashionable accessories.

The great Chicago Fire of 1871 destroyed the store, but because most of the valuable merchandise had been locked in a fireproof vault, the business survived. It also survived the depression of 1893 when, through Charles Peacock's personal sacrifice and integrity, the store's debts were settled without lowering the quality of merchandise or the service for which the store was known.

In 1927, Peacock's moved to its present location at State and Monroe Streets, an elegant store featuring bronze doors emblazoned with a peacock and a green marble interior.

In 1970, a major Peacock's tradition ended when opals were sold for the first time, breaking the 133-year-old ban imposed by Elijah Peacock, who believed opals brought bad luck.

"Snowflake"

John-John's sterling "Snowflake" for 1978, a three-dimensional, twelve-pointed, sterling-silver design with a "spoked-wheel" center, was issued by the Dayton-Hudson Jewelers through Caldwell's, J. B. Hudson, J. Jessop & Sons, Shreve's, Charles W. Warren, and Peacock. It has John–John's hallmark and is dated 1978. Dimensions: 3 ″ h x 2¾″ w. Issue price: $20.00.

These same stores carry all of the John-John ornaments that are still available and not exclusive, distributed to them by Dayton Hudson Jewelers.

Halls of Kansas City
(Division of the Hallmark Greeting Card Co.)

The beginning of Halls' retail store (division of Hallmark Card Company) dates to the summer of 1913 when Joyce C. Hall arranged for a single showcase in the lobby of the Gordon and Koppel building on Walnut St., in Kansas City, Missouri. On display in the case were samples of the "paper craft and postcard" line being sold throughout Kansas, Missouri, and Nebraska by Hall Brothers. The Hallmark Card Company was founded in 1910 by Joyce Hall.

Fine social stationery was sold and hurried across the street to Smith-Pierce Engraving Company or upstairs to the Burke Nelson Engraving Company. At both places, stationery, sonal paper items were embossed from steel dies sonal paper items were embossed from steel dyes or printed or hand-illuminated from copper plates and returned to the tiny gift shop to be picked up by the purchaser.

The retail store figured prominently in launching wrapping papers for gift decorations. R. B. Hall, an elder brother who had joined Joyce Hall in 1911, carried some white tissue to the 113 East 11th store in the mid-1920s for use in protecting fragile gifts. He decided to put some of the paper on the counter to see if it would sell as a decoration and for wrapping boxes. The paper sold well, and red and green

Dayton Hudson Jeweler's Snowflake 1978
PHOTO BY KEVIN NASH

tissues were added later. A year later, Hall brothers began selling lined envelopes and the colorful papers used as linings were put on the counters and proved to be the beginning of the decorated gift paper market.

Halls was primarily established as a retail testing laboratory for greeting cards, and it continues to serve the purpose even today. All of the 12,000-odd greeting cards, gift wraps, and other products created annually by the parent company are offered for sale at both Halls' stores in what are probably the most complete greeting card departments in the world.

The first advertising ever done was in the year 1914 in the *Kansas City Star*. The ad read: "Social Stationery—the most complete line of Crane's high-grade stationery ever shown in Kansas City—Hall's Craft Gift Shop." At the bottom of the ad, in bold type, it said: "Greeting Cards For All Occasions." In 1964, Halls opened a dramatic new speciality store of twenty-one shops, boutiques, and galleries on Kansas City's famed

Country Club Plaza, representing a singular concept of retail merchandising and architecture. A companion to Halls in downtown Kansas City, this specialty shop was the parent company, Hallmark Cards, Inc. Halls selected the interior design firm of Paul Laszlo, Beverly Hills, California, to create the elegant interior that is rich with materials from Italy, Spain, Mexico, Thailand, and other sources, both foreign and domestic. (The Laszlo team has created interiors for such establishments as Saks Fifth Ave., the Beverly Hills Hotel, and for individuals such as Sonja Henie, Barbara Hutton, William Wyler, Gloria Vanderbilt, and many other national celebrities.)

In the early 1970's, Halls built in Kansas City the beautiful, fashionable "Crown Center" of shops, hotels, theatres, garage parking arcades, restaurants, and other businesses in a multilevel futuristic design. This fine old firm actually led the sterling Christmas tree ornament business back in 1964 with a bell and has since had other ornaments designed exclusively for them and carries most of the other manufacturers' ornaments. Deanie Olinger, Halls' silver buyer, informed me that ornaments are one of the biggest in sales for her.

"Bell" 1971–1978

Prior to 1971, the Halls' "Bell" was produced by the Webster Company. When Webster was sold and the John-John Company was established in 1971, they were contracted to produce the Halls' "Bell." The "Bell" is an open sterling silver one with gold wash inside. In the old school-bell design, it is annual, dated, engraved with "Christmas," stamped with John-John's hallmark, marked "sterling," and is exclusively, Halls of Kansas City, Missouri. It will be issued through Halls annually. 2½″ high. Issue price: $20.00.

149

Hall of Kansas City Annual Bell 1971
PHOTO BY KEVIN NASH

1977 Second Edition Christmas Star by Halls of Kansas City
PHOTO BY KEVIN NASH

"Candy Canes" 1971–1978

Another Halls exclusive made prior to 1971 by Webster, now made by John-John is the "Candy Cane." It is a thick strip of sterling silver, twisted like ribbon candy that curves at one end like "Candy Canes." A small, charm-like disc that is dated and engraved with "Christmas" is attached at the end of the curve. It is marked "sterling" and hallmarked by John–John. It is 5″ long and is available through Halls, annually. Issue price: $20.00.

"Christmas Star" Collection (1976—first edition)

The first annual, limited-edition "Christmas Star" for Halls was designed by John Glisson for the bicentennial year, 1976. A variation of John-John's 1975 star became the exclusive design of Halls' 1976. All stars are three-dimensional. This edition is dated and limited by the design of it for that year only. It is marked "Halls Sterling" and is no longer available. Issue price: $20.00.

"Christmas Star" Collection (1977—second edition)

"Christmas Star," the 1977 second edition, Halls' exclusive and marked so. It is dated and the same size and basic design of the first edition, only the center flower design is different. It is no longer available. Issue price: $20.00.

"Christmas Star" Collection (1978—third edition)

The 1978 "Christmas Star" of Halls' limited-edition, annual Christmas star collection is distinguished from the previous stars by its date 1978 marking and change in its center design. An exclusive of and available only through Halls of Kansas City. Issue price: $20.00.

1977 First Edition Snowflake by Halls of Kansas City
PHOTO BY KEVIN NASH

"Snowflake Collection"
(1977—first edition)

The 12-pointed, 3-dimensional "Snowflake" created by John-John and issued by them in 1975 became a first edition of Halls' "Snowflake" Collection" in 1977 by a contract between the two companies to simply mark it "Halls Sterling 1977." Issued by Halls that year at $20.00, it is no longer available. 3″ high.

"Snowflake"
(1978—second edition)

The "Snowflake," 1978 second edition for Halls' is the same as 1977 except for a different center design. It is the same size (3″), and is marked "Halls Sterling—1978." Issue price: $20.00.

Halls of Kansas City Hallmark Company's Reindeer Mobile Ornament
PHOTO BY KEVIN NASH

151

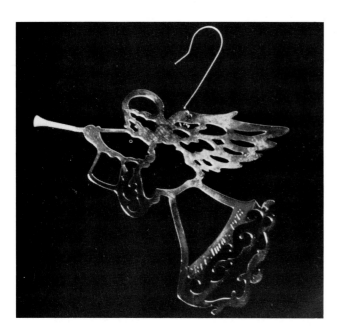

Halls of Kansas City's 1978 Angel
PHOTO BY KEVIN NASH

"Angel" 1978

A flat cut-out, sterling "Angel" blowing a horn was created by John–John in 1978. The profiled "Angel," with her horn raised toward the sky, appears to be floating on clouds; her wings are cut out in feathered effect. She is haloed and the border of her skirt is engraved with "Christmas —1978." From tip of horn to bottom of cloud, she is 3¾″ h.

(Halls also carries John–John's "Bell," "Twelve Days of Christmas" and "Holly Sprig," though not exclusively.)

"The Little Drummer Boy" (1979 — first edition)

For $60 in 1979, Halls of Kansas City made available an adorable, three-dimensional, sterling silver "Little Drummer Boy." The antiqued, hand-finished ornament was designed by Mary Hamilton and crafted by skilled British silversmiths in exquisite detail. The date is inscribed on the drum. It is the first of an annual series of ornaments that will symbolize the "12 Days of Christmas."

The 2¾″ ornament has a 15″, red silk cord attached for display. Issue price: $60.00.

This ornament was advertised in *The Wall Street Journal* and sold out at Halls in Kansas City only. I'm looking forward to the eleven other versions of Halls' "12 Days of Christmas."

⎯ 20 ⎯
The Janna Collection Mexico

The Janna Collection, according to Brenda Vier-thaler of Sterling Imports of Butler, Pennsylvania, is one designed by an American woman named Janna and handcrafted at her shop in Mexico. Sterling Imports carries a complete line of the Janna ornaments, as do many fine department stores. The Janna ornaments are all sterling and marked "Sterling, Janna, and Mexico." Brenda Vierthaler tells me that there are more than 150 different ornaments in the "Janna Collection"—the largest collection to date. In my collection are:

1. "A Partridge in a Pear Tree." A thin triangular ornament showing a partridge and six pears in a tree. Issue price: $24.00.
2. An adorable dressed-up "Snowman." Issue price: $19.50.
3. A "Swirled Angel." Issue price: $19.50.

Janna of Mexico   Snowman
PHOTO BY KEVIN NASH

153

— 21 —
The Frank Lewis Collection

A three-way combination of Luther Bookout, designer, Frank Lewis of the Royal Ruby Red Fresh Fruit Mail Order Company in Alamo, Texas, and the Gorham Silver Company is responsible for one of the most beautiful, the most limited collections I have ever seen.

Mr. Bookout, holding several degrees in fine arts and sculpturing, for over thirty years has earned his living in the commercial art field while yearning for the opportunity to get back to his first love, sculpturing. A very wise Mr. Frank Lewis realized Mr. Bookout's talents (he produced the Ruby Red Catalogs for Mr. Lewis) and commissioned him to design annual limited Christmas ornaments to be made by the Gorham Silver Company.

The collection was sold by subscription only and is limited to "Ninety Eight Hundred" annually!

The subscriber was assigned a number as orders were received on a "first-come" basis. I am number "eight." That number was permanently assigned to me, so each year my ornament will bear my number, "8 of 9800," the artist's name; Luther Bookout, and Gorham's markings.

Each ornament weighs a full troy ounce of sterling and is elegantly packaged in a presentation case.

Christmas Angel 1975 First Edition by Frank Lewis
PHOTO BY FRANK LEWIS

The Madonna 1977 Third Edition by Frank Lewis
PHOTO BY FRANK LEWIS

A Christmas Angel 1975

"A Christmas Angel" is the first edition, issued in 1975 and is 4½" high. The contemporary-styled angel has a halo, and a hair style frames her "impish" smiling face. Her wings have a feathered effect, her gown lies in folds, and her hands are clasped beneath her chin as if she were praying. A beautiful beginning to a beautiful collection. Issue price: $39.00.

Drummer Boy 1976

My true love is Mr. Lewis' second edition to his collection. Mr. Luther Bookout created a work of art in the 1976 "Drummer Boy." The poor "Drummer Boy" delighted the newborn King in Bethlehem by playing his drum—he could offer no other gift. His ragged clothing and humble expression steals your heart, and he reminds you of every hyperactive, inquisitive little boy you have ever known! Issue price: $39.00.

Mother and Child 1977

Nothing is more precious than a mother's love for her child. A more precious child was never born than Christ our Savior, and that is the subject of the 1977, third issue in this collection. A perfectly sculptured "Mother and Child," Mary's face reveals the tender love for the Infant Jesus she holds in her arms. Issue price: $39.00.

Peace Dove 1978 Fourth Edition by Frank Lewis
PHOTO BY KEVIN NASH

Dove 1978

The 1978 issue will be a "Dove" weighing one full ounce of sterling, created by Luther Bookout, bearing the collector's number and the edition number, and made by Gorham. This collection is a beautiful Christmas tradition, will become a treasured heirloom, and is at the top of my list of favorites. Issue price: $39.00.

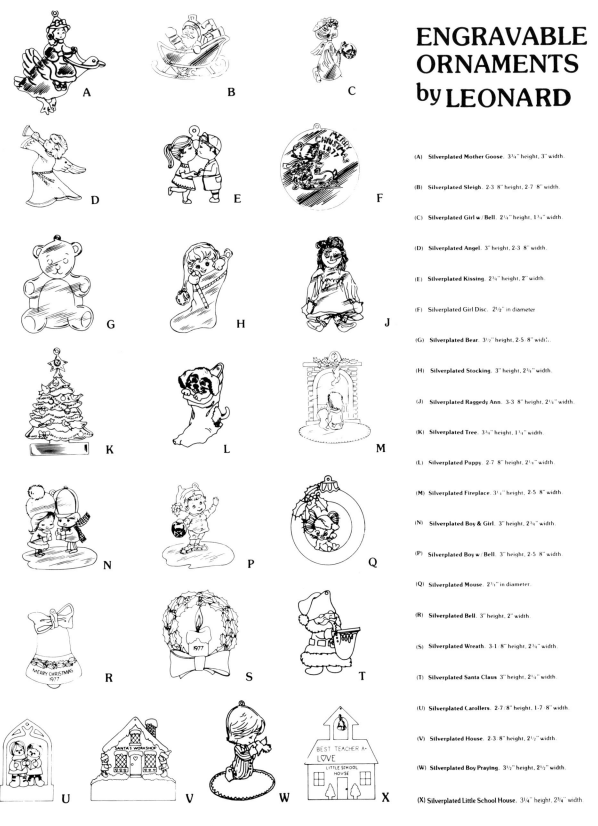

ENGRAVABLE ORNAMENTS
by LEONARD

(A) Silverplated Mother Goose. 3¾" height, 3" width.

(B) Silverplated Sleigh. 2-3/8" height, 2-7/8" width.

(C) Silverplated Girl w/Bell. 2¼" height, 1¾" width.

(D) Silverplated Angel. 3" height, 2-3/8" width.

(E) Silverplated Kissing. 2¾" height, 2" width.

(F) Silverplated Girl Disc. 2½" in diameter

(G) Silverplated Bear. 3½" height, 2-5/8" width.

(H) Silverplated Stocking. 3" height, 2¾" width.

(J) Silverplated Raggedy Ann. 3-3/8" height, 2¼" width.

(K) Silverplated Tree. 3¾" height, 1¾" width.

(L) Silverplated Puppy. 2-7/8" height, 2¼" width.

(M) Silverplated Fireplace. 3¼" height, 2-5/8" width.

(N) Silverplated Boy & Girl. 3" height, 2¾" width.

(P) Silverplated Boy w/Bell. 3" height, 2-5/8" width.

(Q) Silverplated Mouse. 2¾" in diameter.

(R) Silverplated Bell. 3" height, 2" width.

(S) Silverplated Wreath. 3-1/8" height, 2¾" width.

(T) Silverplated Santa Claus 3" height, 2¼" width.

(U) Silverplated Carollers. 2-7/8" height, 1-7/8" width.

(V) Silverplated House. 2-3/8" height, 2½" width.

(W) Silverplated Boy Praying. 3½" height, 2½" width.

(X) Silverplated Little School House. 3¼" height, 2¾" width.

Engravable Ornaments by Leonard Silver Company

O. "Girl Disc"—2½″ Diameter
P. "Raggedy Ann"—3⅜″ × 2¼″
Q. "Fireplace"—3¼″ × 2⅝″
R. "Bear"—3½″ × 2⅝″
S. "Girl-Noel"—3″ × 3″
T. "Stocking"—3″ × 2¾″
U. "Tree"—3¾″ × 1¾″
V. "Santa Claus"—3″ × 2¼″
W. "Bell"—3″ × 2″
X. "Girl with Bell"—2¼″ × 1¾″
Y. "Kissing"—2¾″ × 2″

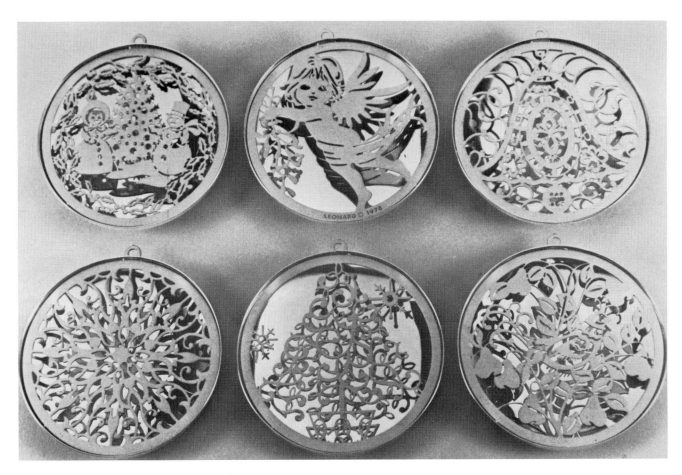

Leonard Silver Company's Trim-A-Tree 1978 Collection
PHOTOS BY LEONARD SILVER COMPANY

23

James Avery Craftsman, Inc. Collection

From the time of his own graduation until 1954, James Avery taught design in universities in Iowa, Colorada and Minnesota. In 1950 he began to think of leaving the teaching profession. Although stimulating, working with college-aged people was quite a drain on his own energy and ideas, so he decided to leave the academic community and concentrate on his own work. At about the same time he returned to the church, after years of being what he terms a "defensive agnostic." This renewed Christian commitment is the reason so much of his work bears its symbolism.

He started working in a garage in Kerrville, with a capital investment of about $250. With this money he built a workbench and bought some hand tools, working alone for the first three years. In his own words, "Ideas, plenty of hard work and prayers (not necessarily in that order) were the rule of each day." The basic elements that he put into his jewelry were simplicity of design, integrity of structure and fine craftsmanship. His customers were impressed enough to spread the word and create more and more customers. People would come to Kerrville for the jewelry, and inquiries and orders came through the mail. Until five or six years ago, word of mouth was the only form of advertising James Avery used.

In 1957, he hired his first employee. By 1968 he had over 25 employees and he moved to his present location at harper Road, about 4½ miles from Kerrville. There are now plants in Com-
fort, where about thirty employees do finishing work on jewelry, and in Fredricksburg, also with about 30 employees, where the casting operations have been consolidated.

The Kerrville complex has ten major buildings and about 150 employees, in departments ranging from marketing and data processing, to design and production. There is also a retail shop in the main building, which has been followed in recent years by a dozen more James Avery Craftsman shops in California, Oklahoma, Louisiana and Texas. There are also over 1,200 dealers throughout the country—churches, religious organizations, bookstores, boutiques and gift shops. Thus, James Avery jewelry has spread from a garage in Kerrville, across the country and as far as Alaska and Hawaii.

In 1974, the first Christmas ornaments by James Avery Craftsman were made available to the public.

The James Avery Craftsman Christmas Tree Ornaments are original, copyrighted designs stamped from sheet silver, carefully inspected and buffed to a high polish.

All are still being made except the following five ornaments, which were made in 1974 only, and were handcut from sheet silver:

Camel, $17.00 in 1974
Tricycle, $21.50 in 1974
Poinsettia, $24.00 in 1974
Angel with star, $17.50 in 1974
Small Angels with star, $15.00 in 1974

Trumpet Christmas Tree Ornament 1974

"With trumpets and sound of cornets make a joyful noise before the Lord, the King." At Christmastime, the trumpet is accepted as a symbol of joy and celebration. Dimensions: 3½″ x 3″. Issue price: $10.00.

Singing Angel Christmas Tree Ornament 1974

Angels have special significance at Christmastime, because it was their joyful duty to announce the coming of Christ, as well as His arrival. Dimensions: 3⅛″ x 3⅛″. Issue price: $22.50.

Star Christmas Tree Ornament 1974

The Star of Jacob, the Star of Bethlehem, the Star in the East, the Christmas Star—all have reference to that single star that led the wise men to worship Christ. Dimensions: 3⅞″ x 4″. Issue price: $15.00.

Reindeer Christmas Tree Ornament 1974

Although the reindeer is generally considered a secular symbol at Christmastime it is also significant as a religious symbol. Referred to as the hart, or stag, in *Psalms*, the reindeer has come to typify piety and religious aspiration. Dimensions: 2¾″ x 3⅞″. Issue price: $10.00.

Dove Christmas Tree Ornament 1974

The dove, being a symbol for the Holy Spirit, is also accepted as a symbol for the miraculous conception of Jesus Christ. Dimensions: 3⅜″ x 3⅜″. Issue price: $12.50.

Toy Horn Christmas Tree Ornament 1974

The toy horn represents the joy of children at Christmastime. Dimensions: 3⅝″ x 2½″. Original price: $17.50.

James Avery Craftsman, Inc. Trumpet
PHOTO BY JAMES AVERY

James Avery Craftsman, Inc. Singing Angel
PHOTO BY JAMES AVERY

James Avery Craftsman, Inc. Star
PHOTO BY JAMES AVERY

James Avery Craftsman, Inc. Reindeer
PHOTO BY JAMES AVERY

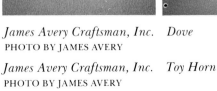

James Avery Craftsman, Inc. Dove
PHOTO BY JAMES AVERY

James Avery Craftsman, Inc. Toy Horn
PHOTO BY JAMES AVERY

"Christmas Tree" Christmas Tree Ornament 1975

The cedar tree is a symbol of Christ. The prophet Ezekiel used it as a symbol of the Messiah and His Kingdom. The use of the Christmas tree as a symbol for Christ at Christmastime began in the 16th century with Martin Luther, the German Protestant leader of church reform. Dimensions: 3⅞" x 4". Issue price: $15.00.

Camel Christmas Tree Ornament 1977

The camel represents one of the religious traditions of Christmas. the three wise men traveled on camels in their quest for the Christ Child, to worship Him and bring him gifts. Dimensions: 3-5/16" x 3⅝". Issue price: $15.00.

Bell Christmas Tree Ornament 1977

The bell was used to call people to worship. The bells of Christmas call people to celebrate the birth of the Christ Child. Dimensions: 3-5/16" x 3⅝". Issue price: $15.00.

James Avery Craftsman, Inc.   Christmas Tree
PHOTO BY JAMES AVERY

James Avery Craftsman, Inc.   Camel
PHOTO BY JAMES AVERY

James Avery Craftsman, Inc.   Bell
PHOTO BY JAMES AVERY

Beatitudes Star Christmas Tree Ornament 1978

The eight-pointed star is symbolic of the eight Beatitudes of Christ's Sermon on the Mount. The beatitudes are blessings, and surely Christmas is the most blessed of holidays. Dimensions: 5" x 3 13/16". Issue price: $20.00.

Nativity Christmas Tree Ornament 1978

Christmas is the celebration of the birth of Christ. This ornament shows the Christ Child in the manger, with the Star of Bethlehem, above, pointing the way. Dimensions: 3½" x 3½". Issue price: $20.00.

Drummer Boy Christmas Tree Ornament 1979

This ornament is a silhouette of the humble little drummer boy of Bethlehem. Dimensions: 4" x 2". Issue price: $30.00.

Snowflake Christmas Tree Ornament 1979

This intricately cut snowflake has a highly polished finish that will sparkle on the Christmas tree. Dimensions: 3¾" x 3¼". Issue price: $30.00.

Partridge in a Pear Tree Christmas Tree Ornament 1979

This graceful tree ornament is a representation of the well-loved Christmas carol. Dimensions: 3⅝" x 3¼". Issue price: $30.00.

James Avery Craftsman, Inc.   *Beatitudes Star*
PHOTO BY JAMES AVERY

James Avery Craftsman, Inc.   *Nativity*
PHOTO BY JAMES AVERY

James Avery Craftsman, Inc.   *Drummer Boy*
PHOTO BY JAMES AVERY

James Avery Craftsman, Inc.   *Snowflake*
PHOTO BY JAMES AVERY

James Avery Craftsman, Inc.
Partridge
PHOTO BY JAMES AVERY

___24___
Smaller Collections and Companies

Bridalana
Cariter Mint of Canada
Downs Collectors Showcase
Marius Hansen, Ltd.
Leonore Doskow, Inc.
Shreve Crump & Low
F. B. Rogers Silver Co.
Determined Productions, Inc.
Candles

Bridalane
1977 Collection

Bridalane introduced in 1977, three semiround ornaments, designed exclusively by James B. Fisher, Jr., of St. Louis, Missouri, and made in Spain. Bridalane promised on their brochure that this series will continue. The collection consisted of:

A. "Santa Claus"—2¼″ h
B. Angel with Harp—2½″ h
C. Jack-in-the-Box—3″ h
Issue prices unknown to the author.

The Cartier Mint of Canada

"Sleigh" 1974

This Mint produced a hexagon-shaped sterling ornament, a "Sleigh," in 1974. It is marked "LC" on the runner of the sleigh and a wreath is designed on the back. Dimension: 2 3/16″. Issue price: $50.00.

Downs Collectors Showcase

"Snowflake" 1976

Down's Collectors Showcase entry into the silver ornament scene was in 1976. The first annual

Santa's Sleigh by The Cartier Mint of Canada
DRAWING COURTESY OF STEVE SMITH

sterling-silver "Snowflake" was made for Down's by a firm in West Germany. It is 2″ in diameter, see-through design, and has the year 1976 in the center. Issue price was $15.95. This is a very thin but pretty ornament. No longer available; collection discontinued.

A new collection is expected from Downs in 1979. This company of fine, beautiful collectibles moved from Evanston, Illinois, to Milwaukee, Wisconsin, in 1978 in an expansion program. They offered many collector items through a large mailing of their catalog.

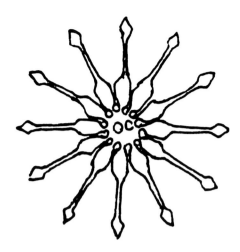

Snowflake by Downs Collector Showcase
DRAWING COURTESY OF STEVE SMITH

Marius Hansen, Ltd.

"Reindeer Bell" 1977

This firm offered a sterling "Bell," complete with decorations of six reindeer in 1977. Advertised in leading magazines, this ¾″ × ¾″ × ½″ "Bell" was considered quite expensive for its size. This Finnish-made ornament, marked 92SS is not dated. Issue price: $32.50.

*Leonore Doskow, Inc.
of Montrose, New York*

Lenore Doskow has developed a booming business serving speciality shops, department stores, and jewelers whose customers seek that "Special and Different" gift of sterling silver, such as cookie cutters, thumb tacks, tooth picks, measuring spoons, yo-yos, and almost anything else you can imagine!

As a young teenager she was introduced to "silver crafting" at summer camp, and responding to her request, she was given a set of jeweler's tools by her parents. The first item she designed and made was sold—a napkin ring. Upon graduation from Bryn Mawr College, she received a scholarship to and studied at the Sorbonne in Paris, continuing her education in the history of art.

The seventy employees at Doskow's had no previous craft skills; they learned by doing and were taught by what I consider "A Master of the Art," Mrs. Doskow, assisted by her husband, David Doskow.

The 130-page catalog carries over 2,000 beautiful items to every state in the U.S. and to foreign countries—including Sterling Silver Christmas Ornaments!

To date there are four ornaments in the Doskow collection. The ornaments are marked "sterling" and carry the hallmark of Lenore Doskow Inc. They were first made in 1971, are not limited, and can be dated on request.

"Christmas Bell"

The sterling silver, traditionally shaped "Bell" is engraved, "Christmas" and the year date, has a clapper, and has a ring on top for hanging. Issue price: $20.00.

"Christmas Tree"

Leonore Doskow's "Christmas Tree" is in a cookie cut-out fashion. The three-tiered sterling tree has a base on trunk, a loop on top for hanging, and is decorated with a "ball" hanging

A Christmas Bell by Leonore Doskow
PHOTO BY LEONORE DOSKOW

171

from the bottom of the center tier that says "Christmas" and whatever date (year) you would like. Price, $20.00.

"Poinsettia"

An eight-petal "Poinsettia" flower with each petal shaped slightly differently and connected at their tips to a sterling, framing circle. The "Poinsettia" is centered with four sterling berries and has its own hook for hanging. Price $20.00. Non-limited.

"Holly Leaves & Berries"

A sterling circle with an arched band across the top has two graceful "Holly Leaves" droping down and connecting to the bottom of the circle. Their prickly points are connected in the center and to the sides of the circled ornament.

Each leaf has a cluster of three sterling "Berries." Price, $20.00.

A Christmas Tree by Leonore Doskow
PHOTO BY LEONORE DOSKOW

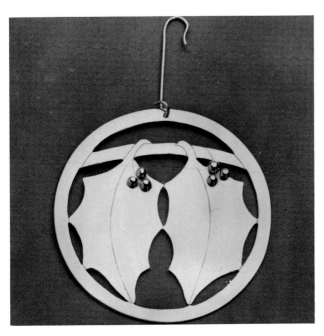

Holly and Berries by Leonore Doskow
PHOTO BY LEONORE DOSKOW

Poinsettia by Leonore Doskow
PHOTO BY LEONORE DOSKOW

172

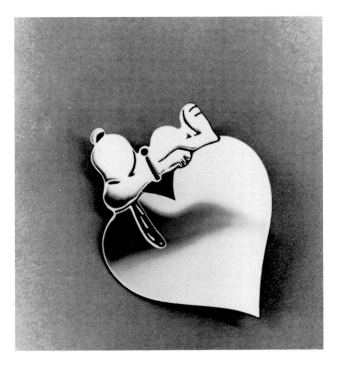

Determined Production's Snoopy

Snoopy On A Heart by Determined Production

A Sterling Silver Snoopy by Determined Production

Snowflakes Made in Germany
PHOTO BY KEVIN NASH

*Candles
(Manufacturer Unknown)*

Knowing of my constant quest for sterling, silver-plated, and vermeil Christmas ornaments and not desirous of duplicating any in my collection, my former mother-in-law gave to me for Christmas in 1977, seven darling little, unmarked, silver-plated candle ornaments.

The candles are 3¾″ tall including the flame that is centered in a 1½″ "haloed glow." It is molded with a "dripping" effect, is three-dimensional, has a hanging loop on top, and is coated to resist tarnish.

Each candle came in its own red felt bag tucked in a little red box. The only clue I have is that they were purchased at Lord and Taylor's in the special "Christmas Ornament—Christmas Card and Giftware Section." I love them!

178

Silverplated Heart-Manufacturer Unknown
PHOTO BY KEVIN NASH

1977 Candle-Manufacturer Unknown
PHOTO BY KEVIN NASH

25

How to Start Your Collections and Where to Find and Buy Them

Now that you have read and hopefully enjoyed my book, you are well acquainted with not only the vast number of ornament collections, designs, issue dates, and prices but also the manufacturers and companies responsible for them.

Collecting for me has been a six year, year round, expensive hobby or a vocation. The major reason is that I did not have a book such as this to tell me who made what, when, why, how, and/or where. I had to seek dealers all over the country to find past issues, and when I found they existed, I found also that, if the dealer had it, it could cost as much as a monthly house mortgage in Fairfield County—in Connecticut!

This chapter is to aid collectors or future collectors by showing what has been issued, by whom, dates and prices of issues, and an idea of what to expect to pay for them today. Also, the descriptions and designers, the metals (silver plate, vermeil, and/or sterling), dimensions, and illustrations are addressed so that one can systematically go about collecting at the dealers listed and/or your local department stores, jewelers, and gift shops.

Some publications are available by subscription that can prove invaluable to the collector, such as the Metropolitan Museum of Art's catalog, where in the fall issues or Christmas catalog they make their ornaments available.

The American Heritage Publishers make theirs available through their publications and catalog, the Smithsonian through the *Smithsonian Magazine* and the *Antique Trader,* one of the largest weekly newspapers of antiques and collectibles of all kinds. In the *Trader,* ornaments are advertised by many dealers all year long. Many dealers have periodic mailings of their own collector *News Letters* to their customers and club members. The Mint's ornaments are sold by subscriptions. The names, addresses, and telephone numbers of where to buy will be listed at the end of this chapter.

There are many ways to collect ornaments to enjoy now, to give as gifts, as well as to create family heirlooms and make a legend of yourself for generations to come in your own family. If you are interested in investing, collecting these ornaments can be one of the best investments you can make.

The fun of collecting for me has been in locating an ornament after months of searching to fill that open year in my collection, or going all-out to collect a set that was closed before I realized it existed, such as two collections that have eluded me, the Metropolitan Museum of Art's "Stars" and "Snowflakes" and the Lincoln Mint's "Holiday Charmers." I won't rest until I have them. The ornaments are like "my children" and I cannot have any of them missing.

180

In serious collecting one should concentrate on completing the set of whatever collection(s) you decide on. Since the first edition is almost always the hardest to find and the most expensive to buy, if you can afford it buy it when you find it—it will probably be sold if you wait and it increases in cost by the day—so get it out of the way. There are some ornaments that are not first editions and that for a number of reasons become rare or hard to find also, so seek those out first too, such as Towle's second edition and fifth edition (the "Five Golden Rings" with five gold rings on the sterling ornament) and the Wallace's 1976 "Bell" that disappeared from stores long before Christmas in 1976.

It is best to try for the ornaments that were introduced in 1976, 1977, and/or 1978 to complete the sets with less dollar output.

Another way to collect is in a specific theme, for example, "Snowflakes." Many companies have their own collections and interpretations so no two will be alike. Gorham, Reed and Barton, the Metropolitan Museum of Art, International, Oneida, Danbury Mint, John-John, General Mills, and Halls of Kansas City all have "Snowflakes." You can have a tree of silver "Bells," "Stars," or "Toys," and there are seven collections of the "Twelve Days of Christmas," all completely different!

With this book and some of the tips I have given plus the dealers listed and publications, you can have a much easier way of deciding what to collect, where you may possibly find them, and ideas of what you will have to pay. It is important to keep all original boxes or cases ornaments are packaged in from the manufacturer and the "Romance" or Legend" (the little descriptive card accompanying the ornament), retain the protective bags some ornaments are placed in, and any other original packaging. Keep records of your original purchase prices. Remember, by the time this book is in your hands, all prices have increased because of supply and demand—more collectors are born each day.

Enjoy!

Stores and Dealers

Zantow-Ferguson Inc.
Carol Ferguson Vesely - Jimmy Hughes & Sarah Hughes
(203) 323-2233
71 Broad St.
Stamford, Connecticut 06901
Carries most collections.

David Harvey Jewelers
The Roseman's
(203) 838-0627
51 Wall St.
Norwalk, Connecticut 06850
Carries most current ornaments.

Albatross Antiques, Inc.
Roy & Nan Shoults
(612) 439-6993
5901 Omaha Avenue, North
Stillwater, Minnesota 55082
Carries most collections.

Rogers & Co. of Mansfield Inc.
Kathy Musille
(419) 522-1561
248 W. Park Ave.
Mansfield, Ohio 44902
Carries most collections.

The Lower Plate
Barbara Weirich
(405) 751-8637
PO Box 20013
Oklahoma City, Oklahoma 73120
Carries most collections.

Watson's
(219) 654-3550 or (800) 348-2530
135 East Michigan St.
New Carlisle, Indiana 46552
Carries some collections.

Tankes Jewelers
(716) 852-4114
569 Main St.
Buffalo, New York 14203

Halls Plaza
Deanie Olinger, Buyer
(816) 274-3244
211 Nichols Rd.
Kansas City, Missouri 64112

Downs Collectors Showcase
Cathy Cohen, Catalog Mgr.
(414) 545-4200
6040 W. Beloit Rd.
Milwaukee, Wisconsin 53219
Has catalog mailings.

Cazenovia Abroad Ltd.
Pat Trush
(315) 655-3433
67 Albany St.
Cazenovia, New York 13055
Cazenovia collection only.

Sterling Imports
Brenda Vierthaler
(412) 586-6366
174 East Airport Rd.
Butler, Pennsylvania 16001
Carries Jana collection only.

Kruckemeyer and Cohn Jewelers
Mrs. Joanne Levi (Collector's Dept.)
(1-800) 457-3536 or (812) 464-9111
309-311 Main St.
Evansville, Indiana 47708
Carries most collections.

Metropolitan Museum of Art (Their collections
only)
Fifth Ave. at 82nd St.
New York, New York 10028

Mints

The Danbury Mint (Mint's collections only)
47 Richards Ave.
Norwalk, Connecticut 06856

The Franklin Mint Corp. (Mint's collections
only)
Franklin Center, Pennsylvania 19091

The Lincoln Mint (Mint's collections only)
One South Wacker Dr.
Chicago, Illinois 60606

The Hamilton Mint
210 North Main St.
Jacksonville, Florida 32202
(904) 358-4445

Publications

The Antique Trader Weekly (Antique Newspaper)
P.O. Box 1050
Dubuque, Iowa 52001

Smithsonian (Monthly magazine—their
collections only)
900 Jefferson Drive
Washington, D.C. 20560

American Heritage Publishing Co. Inc. (Their
collection only)
Catalog Department
P.O. Box 1776
Marion, Ohio 43302

—26—
Displaying & Caring for Your Collection

Displaying

The most obvious way of displaying Christmas tree ornaments would be hanging on the branches of a Christmas tree. However, sterling-silver, plated, and vermeil ornaments are not ordinary ornaments.

Since (unlike the multicolor balls and figurines normally used) these ornaments are basically one color, creativity is needed to *highlight* without *overshadowing* them. You may want to use a *green* tree, a *flocked* tree, or a *colored* tree. The use of colored ribbons to tie them on the branches is very effective. I used (in 1977) a white tree, tied the ornaments with white ribbons, and used the soft pink twinkle lights on white cord for Christmas. The white ribbons blended in with the white branches and made the ornaments *stand out*. The small pink lights caused the tree to have a "glow" that reflected on the shining ornaments. WALLA!!!
The many other ways I have found for decorating with my ornaments are:

1. My cocktail table centerpiece: A large crystal bowl, filled with greenery—piled high on top with Wallace sleigh bells and Reed & Barton's holly balls with bunches of red holly balls (artifical) tucked "here and there."
2) Wreath: *inside* my door. Suspended Santa (Gorham's) on invisible cord from the top of wreath to center.

An ornament display arrangement
PHOTO BY KEVIN NASH

183

A Reed and Barton "Holly Ball" and Wallace Silversmith "Sleigh Bell" Arrangement with a Star by John John.
PHOTO BY KEVIN NASH

An Arrangement of Snowflakes for wall or door
PHOTO BY KEVIN NASH

3) Dining table centerpiece: Styrofoam cone covered with fresh or artificial greenery and holly with small ornaments, all pinned on with florist pins—top cone with star or snowflake.

4) Window dressing: ornaments (variety) suspended at different levels from ceiling on invisible plastic threads.

5. Thanks to a friend and collector, Steve Smith, for some fine suggestions listed here. To quote Steve:

"Gift shops and frame shops usually carry a supply of ready-made shadow boxes that could be used for full-time wall displays of one's collection. If the ready made variety is too small for your series, any good framer can custom make a shadow box to accommodate your desire.

Using a little ingenuity with cloth or decorative backing and the lucite photo cubes that were popular a few years back would also produce a splendid display. The photo cubes come in several different sizes and could house all but the largest of the ornaments listed in this guide. The cubes in turn could be stacked on a shelf or within a cabinet to produce different geometrical designs.

Another method of display, and one that is quite portable and easily stored is the use of Riker (butterfly) mounts. These cardboard and glass-covered display cases also come in many sizes. Most can be purchased in the six- to eight-dollar range from local stamp or coin shops. Should one decide to use this method, use only those mounts that have a cotton display area. Some Riker mounts come with a foam rubber interior that may react with the silver ornaments after contact for a prolonged period.

Of course there are many other ways to display your collection and the reader should be aware that the more exposure the ornaments get, the more cleaning most of them will need. Steps can be taken to reduce this effort by coating the ornaments with several solutions advertised in most of the antique journals or at your local jewelry shop."

The 1978 "Gnome" Collection by The Towle Silversmiths
PHOTO BY TOWLE

Caring for Your Ornaments

There are two disadvantages to collecting these ornaments:

1) You get hooked and it becomes a full time, expensive hobby.
2) Keeping them *clean and shiny!* Some are coated to resist tarnish and how I wish they all were.

As the Christmas season approaches I have to clean my collection so that the facets and designs of my ornaments can be fully appreciated as lights reflect them. You will find that the Wallace bells and Reed & Barton holly balls seem to be *"vermeil"* by the time you dismantle your tree to put it away. My only suggestion is to clean before and after each season's use; some will need more care than others. Make sure that there is a box for every ornament—an ornament for every box as you take your tree apart at the end of the season. Use soft clean cloths—liquid silver polish—plenty of time!

   It Has Been Fun!

_____27_____
Price Guide
Recording Your Collection

It is almost impossible to give definite prices of the ornaments in this book; some of the reasons why are:

a) After each year's production run on the "annual" and/or "limited edition" ornaments, the dyes are retired or destroyed and ornaments (particularly the early ones) must be purchased from the secondary market—meaning a dealer buys from a seller at the seller's asking price and then must pass the increased cost on to the new purchaser, at a profit.

b) The Mints' ornaments are usually subscribed to by those lucky enough to be on "subscriber lists" and many collectors who would like them are not on those lists.

c) Many ornaments are not sold in the usual avenues such as jewelry or department stores.

d) Some ornaments are not sold nationally.

e) Some ornaments are sold by one firm or company, examples, Halls of Kansas City, Neiman Marcus, Horchows, and Dayton Hudson Jewelers. The "prices" listed in this chapter are not current since the value of some of the ornaments seem to increase by the day. Again thanks to Albatross, Zantow Ferguson, The Lower Plate, etc. for their assistance in arriving at the prices listed here as of December, 1978. (FE means "first edition.")

Recording Your Collection

In the price guide there are check boxes ☐ next to each ornament to be checked (√) as you collect. The estimates on values listed can be used for insuring or selling your ornaments. This section is also designed to be a permanent record for the recording of your collection.

Gorham Price Guide

"Sterling Snowflakes"

FE	1970	$150.00	☐
	1971	45.00	☐
	1972	50.00	☐
	1973	45.00	☐
	1974	45.00	☐
	1975	45.00	☐
	1976	45.00	☐
	1977	45.00	☐
	1978	38.50	☐
	1979		☐
	1980		☐
	1981		☐
	1982		☐
	1983		☐
	1984		☐
	1985		☐

"Icicles"

1973	$50.00	☐
1974	50.00	☐

CLOSED

"Unlimited"

1973	Christmas Angel	$40.00	☐
1974	Wiseman	40.00	☐
1975	Drummer Boy	40.00	☐
1976	Snowman	40.00	☐
1977	Santa's Helper	40.00	☐
1978	Waiting for Christmas	40.00	☐
1979	Choirboys	40.00	☐
1980			☐
1981			☐
1982			☐
1983			☐
1984			☐
1985			☐

"Pierced Three Dimensionals"

Turtle	$40.00	☐
Tree	40.00	☐
Ball	40.00	☐
Lantern	40.00	☐
Carousel	35.00	☐
Treasure Chest	35.00	☐
Rocking Horse	35.00	☐
Steam Engine	35.00	☐

"American Heritage"

1973	Mt. Vernon Peace Dove	$50.00	☐
1974	Reindeer	50.00	☐
1975	Angel	50.00	☐
1976	Train	50.00	☐
1977	St. Nick	50.00	☐
1978	Children Round the Tree	50.00	☐
1979	Santa and His Sled	40.00	☐
1980			☐
1981			☐
1982			☐
1983			☐
1984			☐
1985			☐

Towle Price Guide

"Twelve Days of Christmas"

FE	1971	Partridge	Up to $650.00	☐
	1972	Two Turtle Doves	Up to 200.00	☐
	1973	Three French Hens	60.00	☐
	1974	Four Calling Birds	50.00	☐
	1975	Five Golden Rings (all sterling)	45.00	☐
	1975	Five Golden Rings (vermeil rings)	95.00	☐
	1976	Six Geese-A-Laying	47.00	☐
	1977	Seven Swans-A-Swimming	45.00	☐
	1977	Seven Swans-A-Swimming (turquoise center)	50.00	☐
	1978	Eight Maids-A-Milking	40.00	☐
	1979	Nine Ladies Dancing	47.50	☐
	1980			☐
	1981			☐
	1982			☐

CLOSED

"Christmas Melodies"

FE	1978	Silent Night — Holy Night	$40.00	☐
	1979	Deck the Hall with Boughs of Holly	35.00	☐
	1980			☐
	1981			☐
	1982			☐
	1983			☐
	1984			☐
	1985			☐

"Sleigh Bells"

FE	1974	Single	$3.50	☐
	1974	Bells on Leather Strap	25.00	☐
	1979	Christmas Sleigh Bell	15.00	☐

CLOSED

"Towle Discs"

Christmas Tree	$4.00	☐
Bell	4.00	☐
Poinsettia	4.00	☐
Snowflake	4.00	☐
"Twelve Days of Christmas"	$40.00 each	☐
"Twelve Days of Christmas Pendants"	15.00 each	☐

"Santa"

FE	1972	$25.00	☐
	1973	15.00	☐
	1974	10.00	☐
	1975	7.50	☐
	1976	6.50	☐
	1977	5.00	☐
	1978	5.00	☐

CLOSED

Gnomes	$4.00 each	☐
Angel Tree Topping	$20.00	☐
Coach Light Ornament	40.00	☐
Stained Glass Ornament	8.00 each	☐
Photo Cube Ornament	40.00	☐
Snowflake	25.00	☐
Angel	25.00	☐
Christmas Rose	20.00	☐

CLOSED

"American Archives"

1976 Cherub	$7.50	☐
1977 Cherub	8.50	☐
1977 Christmas Tree	7.50	☐
1977 Collection-4 (Single)	4.00	☐
1977 Collection-4 (Double)	8.00	☐

CLOSED

Reed & Barton Price Guide

"Christmas Cross"

FE	1971	$100.00	☐
FE	1971 Gold	110.00	☐
	1972	50.00	☐
	1972 Gold	60.00	☐
	1973	45.00	☐
	1973 Gold	50.00	☐
	1974	45.00	☐
	1974 Gold	50.00	☐
	1975	40.00	☐
	1975 Gold	45.00	☐
	1976	40.00	☐
	1976 Gold	45.00	☐
	1977	40.00	☐
	1977 Gold	45.00	☐
	1978	40.00	☐
	1978 Gold	45.00	☐
	1979	50.00	☐
	1979 Gold	55.00	☐
	1980		☐
	1980 Gold		☐
	1981		☐
	1981 Gold		☐
	1982		☐

1982 Gold		☐
1983		☐
1983 Gold		☐
1984		☐
1984 Gold		☐
1985		☐
1985 Gold		☐

"Stars"

FE	1976	$30.00	☐
FE	1976 Gold	32.00	☐
	1977	27.50	☐
	1977 Gold	30.00	☐
	1978	25.00	☐
	1978 Gold	27.50	☐
	1979	25.00	☐
	1979 Gold	30.00	☐
	1980		☐
	1980 Gold		☐
	1981		☐
	1981 Gold		☐
	1982		☐
	1982 Gold		☐
	1983		☐
	1983 Gold		☐
	1984		☐
	1984 Gold		☐
	1985		☐
	1985 Gold		☐

"Snowflakes" (PAIRS)

1977	$15.00	☐
1977 Gold	20.00	☐
1978	12.00	☐
1978 Gold	15.00	☐
1979	12.50	☐
1979 Gold	13.00	☐

CLOSED

"Twelve Days Bells" (PAIRS)

FE	1977 #1 & 2	$18.50	☐
	1978 #3 & 4	18.50	☐
	1979 #5 & 6	18.50	☐
	1980 #7 & 8	18.50	☐
	1981 # 9 & 10		☐
	1982 #11 & 12		☐

CLOSED

"Tree Castles"

1977 Triangle	$15.00	☐
1977 Large Square	15.00	☐
1977 Small Square	11.00	☐
1978 Choir	10.00	☐
1978 Nativity	10.00	☐
1979 Peace Dove	10.00	☐
1979 Holly	10.00	☐

"Open Bells"

Dated — Undated
Red-Green-Gold-Silver plate
  $5.00 to $7.50 each

"Music Makers"

3 per set	$15.00 per set	☐
CLOSED		

"Holly Balls"

Dated	FE	1976	$25.00	☐
Undated	FE	1976	30.00	☐
		1977	16.00	☐
		1978	15.00	☐
		1979	18.00	☐
		1980		☐
		1981		☐
		1982		☐
		1983		☐
		1984		☐
		1985		☐

"Trim-A-Tree"

"Picture Frames		(Single)		(Pairs)	
FE	1977	$ 7.50	☐	$15.00	☐
FE	1977 Gold	10.00	☐	20.00	☐
	1978	6.00	☐	12.00	☐
	1978 Gold	7.50	☐	15.00	☐
	1979	6.00	☐	12.00	☐
	1979 Gold	6.00	☐	12.00	☐
	1980		☐		☐
	1980 Gold		☐		☐
	1981		☐		☐
	1981 Gold		☐		☐
	1982		☐		☐
	1982 Gold		☐		☐
	1983		☐		☐
	1983 Gold		☐		☐
	1984		☐		☐
	1984 Gold		☐		☐
	1985		☐		☐
	1985 Gold		☐		☐

"Trefoils"

FE	1972	Shepherds Vigil	$50.00	☐
	1973	Gifts of Kings	50.00	☐
	1974	Journey by Starlight	50.00	☐
	1975	First Christmas	50.00	☐
		CLOSED		

"Flowers of Christmas"

FE	1976	Mistletoe	$47.50	☐
	1977	Holly	45.00	☐
		CLOSED		

"Songs of Christmas"

FE	1976	Jingle Bells	$47.50	☐
	1977	Silent Night	45.00	☐
	1978	O' Christmas Tree	40.00	☐
	1979	Joy to the World	35.00	☐
		CLOSED		

"Tiny Tots"

FE	1976	Little Folks (Boy/Girl)	$15.00 each	☐
	1977	Sleepy Heads (Boy/Girl)	15.00 each	☐
		CLOSED		

"Christmas Greenery"

FE	1978	Wreath	$40.00	☐
	1979	Evergreen	30.00	☐
	1980			☐
	1981			☐
	1982			☐
	1983			☐
	1984			☐
	1985			☐

The Kirk/Stieff Price Guide

1972	Christmas Angel	$40.00	☐
1973	Cherub-On-A-Chain	30.00	☐

CLOSED

"Music Bells"

FE	1977	Jingle Bells	$90.00	☐
	1978	White Christmas	30.00	☐
	1979	Deck the Halls (Reindeer)	18.95	☐
	1980			☐
	1981			☐
	1982			☐
	1983			☐
	1984			☐
	1985			☐

The Lincoln Mint Price Guide

"Holiday Charmers" (Collection G-FE set)

Heralding Angel	$75.00	☐
Star of Bethlehem	75.00	☐
Choir Boys	75.00	☐
Santa Claus	75.00	☐
Shepherd	75.00	☐
Christmas	75.00	☐

CLOSED

The Hamilton Mint Price Guide

"Snowflakes"

FE	1976 (1st 4)		$30.00 each	☐
	1977 (2nd 4)		25.00 each	☐

CLOSED

"Twelve Days"

FE	1970	Twelve Days of Christmas Set (sterling)	$250.00 set	☐

CLOSED

"Christmas Carol Collection"

FE	1971	Silent Night	$80.00	☐
	1972	First Noel	80.00	☐
	1973	O' Come All Ye Faithful	80.00	☐
	1974	Hark the Herald Angels Sing	80.00	☐
	1975	O' Little Town of Bethlehem	150.00	☐
	1976	It Came Upon A Midnight Clear	150.00	☐
	1977	O' Holy Night	80.00	☐
	1977	Snowflake Tree Top	120.00	☐
	1977	Christmas Cherub Ornament	95.00	☐
	1978	The Blessing	80.00	☐
	1979	We Three Kings	65.00	☐
	1980			☐
	1981			☐
	1982			☐
	1983			☐
	1984			☐
	1985			☐

The John-John Price Guide

"Twelve Days"

FE	1974	1	Partridges	$75.00	☐
	1976	2	Turtle Doves	75.00	☐
	1978	3	French Hens	70.00	☐
	1980	4	Calling Birds	70.00	☐
	1982	5			☐
	1984	6			☐

CLOSED

1974	Holly Sprig	$50.00	☐
1975	Snowflake	50.00	☐
1975	Holly Bell	50.00	☐
1975	Christmas Star	50.00	☐
1976	Reindeer	50.00	☐
1978	Tree Topping	100.00	☐

Made by John-John Price Guide

Lord & Taylor Bell "First Christmas" 1977 $50.00 ☐
Neiman-Marcus Annual Ball Ornament 1973 to 1978
*No price was available—1978 value (approximately 60.00 each)
Dayton Hudson Jewelers
(Caldwells—J.B. Hudson—J. Jessup & Sons—Shreve's—Charles W. Warren—Peacock Jewelers)
       "Snowflake" 1978 50.00

1971-1978	Bell	$50.00 each	☐
1971-1978	Candy Cane	35.00 each	☐
1978	Angel	25.00	☐

FE	1979	The Little Drummer Boy	$100.00	☐

"Christmas Star Collection"

FE	1976	$50.00	☐
	1977	45.00	☐
	1978	40.00	☐
	1979	25.00	☐
	1980		☐
	1981		☐
	1982		☐
	1983		☐
	1984		☐
	1985		☐

"Snowflake Collection"

FE	1978	$50.00	☐
	1979	25.00	☐
	1980		☐
	1981		☐
	1982		☐
	1983		☐
	1984		☐
	1985		☐

The American Heritage Publishers Price Guide

FE	1972	Mt. Vernon Peace Dove	$75.00	☐
	1973	Christmas Reindeer	70.00	☐
	1974	Christmas Angel	60.00	☐
	1975	Christmas Steam Engine	50.00	☐
	1976	St. Nicholas	45.00	☐
	1977	Children Round the Tree	45.00	☐
	1978	Santa and Sleigh	40.00	☐
	1979	Man on Horseback	38.50	☐
	1980			☐
	1981			☐
	1982			☐
	1983			☐
	1984			☐
	1985			☐

Dove of Peace	$49.00	☐
Bunny	49.00	☐
Teddy Bear	49.00	☐
Porky Pig	49.00	☐
Tiptoe Angel	49.00	☐
Kneeling Angel	72.00	☐
Standing Angel	57.00	☐
Tree Top Angel	57.00	☐
Large Bird Songster	57.00	☐
Fawn	49.00	☐
Snowman Caroller	49.00	☐
Toy Soldier	49.00	☐
Elephant	49.00	☐
Duck	49.00	☐
Cat	49.00	☐
Rooster	49.00	☐
Hatching Chick	49.00	☐
Rocking Horse	72.00	☐
Star	49.00	☐
Donkey	49.00	☐
Conch Shell	49.00	☐
Raggedy Ann	57.00	☐

Leonard Price Guide

1977 Ornaments

Leonard ornaments range in prices from $3.50 to $7.50. They are widely distributed and are found on sale many times—some are expected to increase (very gradually) in value as patterns arc discontinued. For the sake of recording, they are:

Price of each, $3.50

A.	"Boy-Noel"	☐
B.	"House"	☐
C.	"Mouse"	☐
D.	"Boy Disc"	☐
E.	"Angel"	☐
F.	"Sleigh"	☐
G.	"Wreath"	☐
H.	"Mother Goose"	☐
I.	"Puppy"	☐
J.	"Carollers"	☐
K.	"Boy & Girl"	☐
L.	"Boy Praying"	☐
M.	"Best Teacher"	☐
N.	"Boy with Bell"	☐
O.	"Girl Disc"	☐

191

P. "Raggedy Ann" ☐
Q. "Fireplace" ☐
R. "Bear" ☐
S. "Girl-Noel" ☐
T. "Stocking" ☐
U. "Tree" ☐
V. "Santa Claus" ☐
W. "Bell" ☐
X. "Girl with Bell" ☐
Y. "Kissing" ☐

Three Dimensionals, $7.50 each.

1. "Partridge in a Pear Tree" ☐
2. "Snowflake" ☐
3. "Dove" ☐
4. "Santa Claus" ☐
5. "Turtle Doves" ☐
6. "Christmas Tree" ☐
7. "Christmas Gazer"—engraved "Christmas—1977" ☐
8. "Christmas Ball"—engraved "Christmas—1977" ☐
9. "Christmas Bell"—engraved "Christmas—1977" ☐
10. "Clown" ☐
11. "Angel" ☐
12. "Snowman" ☐
13. "Snow-Sled" ☐

"Snoopy Characters"

1977 Collection of the beloved "Snoopy"—$4.00 each.

A. Snoopy—with drum and bird ☐
B. Snoopy—on top of his house ☐
C. Snoopy—hugging the bird ☐
D. Snoopy—opening Christmas package ☐
E. Snoopy—holding a nest with Christmas tree and bird in it ☐
F. Snoopy—with bird and 5 little snowmen ☐

"Stained-Glass Look"

A. "Wreath" in green with red ribbon
   Pewter-look $3.50   ☐
   Silver plate   4.00   ☐
   Gold Finish   5.00   ☐

B. "Christmas Window-Angel" colors: red, blue, green & gold
   Pewter-look $3.00   ☐
   Silver plate   3.50   ☐
   Gold Finish   3.50   ☐

C. "Christmas Window-Elk" colors: red, blue, green & gold
   Pewter-look $3.00   ☐
   Silver plate   3.50   ☐
   Gold Finish   3.50   ☐

D. "Candy Cane" with green bow—colors: red, white & green
   Pewter-look $3.50   ☐
   Silver plate   4.00   ☐
   Gold Finish   4.00   ☐

E. "Christmas Bell/Bow & Holly" colors: red, blue, green & gold
   Pewter-look $3.50   ☐
   Silver plate   4.00   ☐
   Gold Finish   4.00   ☐

F. "Carollers" colors: red, blue, green, gold & white
   Pewter-look $3.50   ☐
   Silver plate   4.00   ☐
   Gold Finish   4.00   ☐

G. "Santa Claus" colors: red, white & gold
   Pewter-look $3.00   ☐
   Silver plate   3.50   ☐
   Gold Finish   3.50   ☐

#1792—A "Clown"
#7158—"Teddy Bear"
#7186—"Boy & Girl"
#7198—"White Snowman"
#7200—"Baby Boy"
#7218—"Santa's Workshop"
#7232—"Boy at Fireplace"
#7154—"Bell"
#7184—"Bell/Bow"
#7190—"Little Red Schoolhouse"
#7194—"Three Yellow Bells"
#7204—"Santa"
#7214—A green "Christmas Tree"

Wallace Price Guide

"Christmas Sleigh Bells"

FE	1971	$500.00	☐
	1972	80.00	☐
	1973	60.00	☐
	1974	45.00	☐
	1975	45.00	☐
	1976	55.00	☐
	1977	22.50	☐
	1978	22.50	☐
	1979	22.50	☐
	1980		☐
	1981		☐
	1982		☐
	1983		☐
	1984		☐
	1985		☐

"Doves"

FE	1971	$150.00	☐
	1972	60.00	☐
	1973	40.00	☐
	1973 Gold	50.00	☐
	1974	40.00	☐
	1974 Gold	45.00	☐
	1975	40.00	☐
	1975 Gold	45.00	☐
	1975 Gold/Silver	45.00	☐
	1976	30.00	☐
	1976 Gold	40.00	☐
	1976 Gold/Silver	35.00	☐
	1977	30.00	☐
	1977 Gold	35.00	☐
	1978	30.00	☐

CLOSED

"Open Bells"

Holly	$20.00	☐
Poinsettia	20.00	☐
Snowflake	20.00	☐

The Metropolitan Museum of Art Price Guide

"Snowflake Collection"
(Sterling)

FE	1971	$100.00	☐
	1972	70.00	☐
	1973	60.00	☐
	1974	50.00	☐
	1975	40.00	☐
	1976	35.00	☐
	1977	30.00	☐
	1978	50.00	☐
	1979		☐
	1980		☐
	1981		☐
	1982		☐
	1983		☐
	1984		☐
	1985		☐

"Star Collection" (vermeil)

FE	1972	$60.00	☐
	1973	55.00	☐
	1974	50.00	☐
	1975	45.00	☐
	1976	40.00	☐
	1977	30.00	☐
	1978	25.00	☐
	1979	50.00	☐
	1980		☐
	1981		☐
	1982		☐
	1983		☐
	1984		☐
	1985		☐

"Bells"

FE	1973	Sterling Christ Crib Bell	$ 60.00	☐
	1973	14 kt Gold Christ Crib Bell	200.00	☐
	1974	Furin Bell	60.00	☐
	1975	Katrina	50.00	☐
	1977	Beehive	40.00	☐
	1978	Birdbells	75.00	☐
	1979	Sterling Christ Crib Bell	50.00	☐
	1979	14 kt Gold Christ Crib Bell	150.00	☐
	1979	Furin Bell	75.00	☐
	1980			☐
	1981			☐
	1982			☐
	1983			☐
	1984			☐
	1985			☐

(No bell produced in 1976)

The Smithsonian Price Guide

	1972	Gabriel Angel	$30.00	☐
	1972	Coptic Cross	33.00	☐
	1973	Ethiopian Ceremonial Bell	32.00	☐

Annual Collection

FF	1978	Triton	$40.00	☐
	1980			☐
	1981			☐
	1982			☐
	1983			☐
	1984			☐
	1985			☐

No Triton produced in 1979

The Danbury Mint Price Guide

Annual Ornament

FE	1976	$35.00	☐
	1977	25.00	☐
	1978	20.00	☐
	1979	13.50	☐
	1980		☐
	1981		☐
	1982		☐
	1983		☐
	1984		☐
	1985		☐

FE 1977 Collection-12

Christmas Tree	$25.00	☐
Bell	25.00	☐
Star	25.00	☐
Candle	25.00	☐
Partridge	25.00	☐
Snowman	25.00	☐
Church	25.00	☐
Teddy Bear	25.00	☐
Jingle Bells	25.00	☐
Wreath	25.00	☐
Reindeer	25.00	☐
Snowflake	25.00	☐

CLOSED

1978 Collection-12

Lantern	$20.00	☐
Holly	20.00	☐
Hobby Horse	20.00	☐
Bell & Bow	20.00	☐
Snowflake (#1)	20.00	☐
Drummer Boy	20.00	☐
Snowflake (#2)	20.00	☐
Candy Cane	20.00	☐
Ragdoll	20.00	☐
Poinsettia	20.00	☐
Jack-in-the-Box	20.00	☐
Snowflake (#3)	20.00	☐

CLOSED

1979 Collection-12

Cathedral	$13.50	☐
Lantern	13.50	☐
Tree	13.50	☐
Mistletoe	13.50	☐
Violin	13.50	☐
Poinsettia	13.50	☐
Angels with Harps	13.50	☐
Gift Package	13.50	☐
Candle	13.50	☐
Santa	13.50	☐
Bell	13.50	☐
Chickadees	13.50	☐

CLOSED

Janna Price Guide

Partridge	$25.00	☐
Snowman	20.00	☐
Swirled Angel	20.00	☐

The Frank Lewis Collection Price Guide

FE	1975	Christmas Angel	$100.00	☐
	1976	Drummer Boy	75.00	☐
	1977	Mother & Child	75.00	☐
	1978	Dove	75.00	☐
	1979	Bells of Peace	50.00	☐

CLOSED

The General Mills (by Oneida) Price Guide

1977 Collection-I

Dove	$3.00	☐
Christmas Tree	3.00	☐
Snowflake	3.00	☐
Mother & Child	3.00	☐

1977 Collection-II

Angel	$3.00	☐
Bells	3.00	☐
Poinsettia	3.00	☐
Candles	3.00	☐

The Oneida Price Guide

FE	1973	Joy to the World	$45.00 ☐
	1974	Nativity	45.00 ☐
	1975	Magi	45.00 ☐

CLOSED

"Reindeer Collection"

FE	1974	Cupid	40.00 ☐
	1975	Vixen	40.00 ☐

CLOSED

"Tree Trimmers" 1977 FE

Sleigh	9.00 ☐	Dove	5.50 ☐	Madonna	5.00 ☐
Snowflake	9.00 ☐	Bell	5.50 ☐	Poinsettia	5.00 ☐
Candle	9.00 ☐	Snowflake	5.50 ☐	Holly	5.00 ☐
Partridge	9.00 ☐	Santa	5.50 ☐	Noel	5.00 ☐
Angel	9.00 ☐	Angel	5.50 ☐	Reindeer	5.00 ☐
Joy	9.00 ☐	Tree	5.50 ☐	Sleigh	5.00 ☐

"Tree Trimmer" Sets 1978

Flat Trimmers

Wreath	$12.00 ☐
Holly	12.00 ☐

Interlocking

Bell	$8.00 ☐
Pear	8.00 ☐

Teardrops

Star	$8.00 ☐
Partridge	8.00 ☐
Crown	8.00 ☐
Madonna	8.00 ☐
Candle	8.00 ☐
Joy	8.00 ☐

Mobiles

Christmas Tree	$3.00 ☐
Santa	3.00 ☐
Dove	3.00 ☐
Christmas Ball	3.00 ☐
Christmas Bird	3.00 ☐
Angel	3.00 ☐

Trimmers

Noel	3.00	☐
Madonna	3.00	☐
Reindeer	3.00	☐
Santa	3.00	☐

James Avery Craftsman, Inc. Price Guide

1974	Trumpet	$72.50	☐
1974	Singing Angel	99.50	☐
1974	Star	87.40	☐
1974	Reindeer	91.60	☐
1974	Dove	95.80	☐
1974	Toy Horn	82.60	☐
1975	Christmas Tree	89.80	☐
1977	Camel	79.60	☐
1977	Bell	89.80	☐
1978	Beatitudes Star	80.30	☐
1978	Nativity	88.00	☐
1979	Drummer Boy	80.70	☐
1979	Snowflake	94.70	☐
1979	Partridge	98.90	☐

The first five ornaments made by handcutting from Sheer Silver in 1974 are practically priceless because they were each hand made and are very few in number. They are listed here with a suggestion of what would be reasonable.

Camel	$250.00	☐
Tricycle	250.00	☐
Poinsettia	250.00	☐
Angel with Star	250.00	☐
Small Angel with Star	250.00	☐

Smaller Collections' Price Guide

Bridalane

Santa	$50.00	☐
Angel/Harp	50.00	☐
Jack in the Box	40.00	☐

Cartier Mint (Canada)

1974 Sleigh	$75.00 ☐

Downs Collectors Showcase

FE 1976 Snowflake	$40.00	☐

(only issue—discontinued)

F.B. Rogers Collections 1977

Angel	$4.00	☐
Snowflake	4.00	☐
Rosette	4.00	☐
Christmas Tree	4.00	☐

Merrill
1976 Raggedy Ann $60.00   ☐

1974 Snoopy $60.00   ☐

Wolfpit Enterprises
Joan Walsh Anglund's
Boy $60.00   ☐   Girl $60.00   ☐

Marius Hansen, Ltd.
1977 Reindeer Bell $60.00   ☐

Candle
(Manufacturer Unknown)
1977 $6.00 each   ☐

The "Happy" End

Raggedy Ann by Cazenovia Abroad Ltd.
PHOTO BY KEVIN NASH

197